Slí na Fírinne

Published by Slí na Fírinne Publishing 2006.

British Library Cataloguing in Publication Data.
A CIP catalogue record for this book is available from the British Library.
ISBN 0-9552322-0-1
978-0-9552322-0-6

Design and production by Slí na Fírinne Publishing.
Printed in the Republic of Ireland by Beta Print, Dublin, Ireland.

Slí na Fírinne

JOHN MORIARTY

Slí na Fírinne Publishing

ACKNOWLEDGMENTS

D. H. Lawrence: "It is not easy to fall out of the hands of the living God", Complete Poems Penguin Books. 1993

Edwin Muir: "Horses", Collected Poems, 2nd ed., 1965

W. B. Yeats: "Song of the Wandering Aengus", Selected Poetry, ed. A. Norman Jeffares, Macmillan, 1971

PREFACE

What follows seeks to elaborate an ethos and rule for a Christian monastic hedge school called Slí na Fírinne.

Some of the pieces that go to make up this document have appeared and will appear elsewhere. I am at ease with this. Text and context colour each other and so a text will do something different and will mean something different in the different semantic environments in which it finds itself.

But why such an undertaking, now?

Unlike D.H. Lawrence, I believe that the venture hasn't gone out of Christianity. But this is not a reason for complacency. As I see it, it isn't only the Christian churches that are in trouble. Christianity as a story is in trouble. It is in trouble in its images and in its metaphors. And, even though it ravages me to say so, it is, I fear, in trouble in its central ritual, the Eucharist.

If we do not get the diagnosis right, it is unlikely that we will happen upon the right remedy.

Christ who continues to grow and outgrow among us is the remedy. That and our willingness to grow and outgrow with him.

Christ's life among us didn't come to an end on Ascension Thursday. His thirty three years on Earth isn't the biographical whole story. A pterosaur his or her symbol, the next Evangelist will talk about him all the way back in to the precambrian and yet further back and all the way forward in to our furthest evolutionary future. In consequence of what he undertook to do and underwent in the Karmic Canyon, Jesus is the contemporary of ammonites, of Pontius Pilate and of beings billions of years from now. Neither Christmas nor Ascension Thursday are biographical bounding walls to the one who said, before Abraham was I am.

Much as Merlin founded the Round Table we would found

SLÍ na FÍRINNE

Our hope is that it will be a virtue in the world.

We think of it as the place of our further and final evolution.

Slí na Fírinne

Of someone who has died we say in Irish, tá sé, tá sí, imithe ar shlí na fírinne, meaning that he, that she, has set out on the path or trail of truth. In Irish, the idea is numinous with a sense of final adventure, the adventure of our immortality. This is lost in translation, so it is best to stay with

    Slí na Fírinne

Not of course that we have to wait until we die to set out into

    Slí na Fírinne

Undergoing conception we can if we choose set out into it.
Undergoing birth we can if we choose set out into it.
No matter where we are in the cycles of birth and death we can if we choose set out into it.
Undergoing baptismal assimilation to Christ crossing the Torrent we are, in very deed, choosing to set out into it.
In this house it is how we think of ourselves.
In this house, inheriting our baptism, we set out with Jesus into

    Slí na Fírinne

Call it

Slí na Fírinne

Call it

The Adventure Of Our Immortality

As

Jesus Pioneered It

It began in egressus:

> Et egressus est Jesus cum discipulis suis trans torrentem Cedron.
> And Jesus went forth with his disciples over a torrent called the
> Kedron.
>
> And they came to a place which was named Gethsemane: and he saith
> to his disciples, sit ye here, while I shall pray. And he taketh with him
> Peter and James and John, and began to be sore amazed and to be very
> heavy.

Sore amazed by what he knows.

> What the Psalmist knows he knows;

> > I am fearfully and wonderfully made.

> What Heraclitus knows he knows:

> > You would not find the boundaries of the soul, even by travel-
> > ling along every path, so deep a measure does it have.

> What Jacob Boehme knows, he knows:

> > In man is all whatsoever the sun shines upon or heaven con-
> > tains, also hell and all the deeps.

> What Sir Thomas Browne knows, he knows:

> > There is all Africa and her prodigies in us.

> What William Law knows, he knows:

> > Thy natural senses cannot possess God or unite thee to Him;
> > nay, thy inward faculties of understanding, will and memory,
> > can only reach after God, but cannot be the place of His
> > habitation in thee. But there is a root or depth in thee whence
> > all these faculties come forth as lines from a centre, or as
> > branches from the body of the tree. This depth is called the
> > centre, the fund or bottom of the soul. This depth is called
> > the unity, the eternity – I had almost said the infinity – of thy

soul; for it is so infinite that nothing can satisfy it or give it any rest but the infinity of God.

The time of disputing and speculating upon ideas is short; it can last no longer than whilst the sun of this world can refresh your flesh and blood, and so keep the soul from knowing its own depth or what has been growing in it. But when this is over, then you must know and feel what it is to have a nature as deep and strong and large as eternity.

What William Wordsworth knows, he knows:

> Not chaos, not
> The darkest pit of lowest Erebus,
> Nor aught of blinder vacancy scooped out
> By help of dreams – can breed such fear and awe
> As fall upon us often when we look
> Into our Minds, into the Mind of Man –

What Baudelaire knows, he knows:

> Homme libre, toujours tu cheriras la mer;
> La mer est ton miroir; tu contemples ton ame
> Dans le deroulement infini de sa lame
> Et ton esprit n'est pas un gouffre moins amer.

What Hopkins knows, he knows:

> O the mind, mind has mountains, cliffs of fall
> Frightful, sheer, no-man-fathomed…

What Emerson knows he knows:

> It is the largest part of a man that is not inventoried. He has many enumerable parts: he is social, professional, political, sectarian, literary, in this or that set or corporation. But after the most exhausting census has been made, there remains as much more which no tongue can tell. And this remainder is that which interests.

What Nietzsche discovered, he knows:

> I have discovered for myself that the old human and animal
> life, indeed the entire prehistory and past of all sentient being,
> works on, loves on, hates on, thinks on in me.

What Conrad knows, he knows:

> The mind of man is capable of anything- because everything is
> in it, all the past as well as all the future.

What William James knows he knows:

> The further limits of our being plunge, it seems to me, into an
> altogether other dimension of existence from the sensible and
> the merely understandable.

What D.H. Lawrence knows he knows:

> There is that other universe, of the heart of man
> that we know nothing of, that we dare not explore.
> A strange grey distance separates
> our pale mind still from the pulsing continent
> of the heart of man.
>
> Fore-runners have barely landed on the shore
> and no man knows, no woman knows
> the mystery of the interior
> when darker still than Congo or Amazon
> flow the heart's rivers of fullness, desire and distress.

What Rilke knows he knows:

> However vast outer space may be, yet with all its sidereal
> distances, it hardly bears comparison with the dimension, with
> the depth dimension, of our inner being, which does not even
> need the spaciousness of the universe to be within itself almost
> unfathomable.

A Bright Angel Trail of mahavakyas and to have set deinanthropic foot on it and to have walked down along it, that already is to have found one's way, as Jesus did, to the floor of the Canyon, that already is to be sore amazed and very heavy, already that is

Passion

It is the one, vast, simultaneous adventure of who we phylogenetically and immortally are because as Sir Thomas Browne reminds us:

> There is surely a piece of Divinity in us, something that was before the Elements and owes no homage unto the Sun.

And yes, it is down onto the floor of the Canyon that Jesus has come. And Bright Angel is there and he points to a mirroring rock-pool and Jesus goes down on his knees and he cups his fin-fraught hands into it and when the water in the cup has settled and it too is mirroring the karma of the ages he drinks it. A cup of trembling it is and the very lees of it he drinks, and his dread is that what happened to Nebuchadnezzar might happen to him:

> The same hour was the thing fulfilled upon Nebuchadnezzar: and he was driven from men, and did eat grass as oxen, and his body was wet with the dew of heaven, till his hairs were grown like eagles' feathers, and his nails like birds' claws.

Idumea, in Isaiah's prophetic vision of it, is his dread, his dread that it is a vision of what might happen to his own mind:

> But the cormorant and the bittern shall possess it: the owl also and the raven shall dwell in it: and he shall stretch out upon it the line of confusion, and the stones of emptiness. They shall call the nobles thereof to the kingdom, but none shall be there, and all her princes shall be nothing. And thorns shall come up in her palaces, nettles and brambles in the fortresses thereof: and it shall be an habitation of dragons, and a court for owls. The wild beasts of the desert shall also meet with the wild beasts of the island, and the satyr shall cry to his fellow: the screech owl also shall rest there, and find for herself a place of rest. There shall the great owl make her nest, and lay, and hatch, and gather under her shadow: there shall the vultures also be gathered, every one with her mate.

And the Psalms speak their passions to him, speak calamity to him and hope to him:

> Fearfulness and trembling are come upon me, and horror hath overwhelmed me.
>
> Save me from the lion's mouth, for thou hast heard me from the horns of the unicorns.
>
> Save me, O God, for the waters are come in unto my soul.
>
> Let not the waterflood overflow me, neither let the deep swallow me up, and let not the pit shut her mouth upon me.
>
> I am counted with those that go down into the pit.
>
> Thou hast laid me in the lowest pit, in darkness, in the depths.
>
> O God, thou hast cast us off, thou hast scattered us, thou hast been displeased. O turn thyself to us again. Thou hast made the earth to tremble: thou hast broken it: heal the breeches thereof for it shaketh. Thou hast shewed thy people hard things, thou hast made us to drink the wine of astonishment.
>
> Therefore will not we fear, though the earth be removed, and the mountains be carried into the midst of the sea.
>
> Truly my soul waiteth upon God, from him cometh my salvation.
>
> Our heart is not turned back, neither have our steps declined from thy way, though thou hast sore broken us in the place of dragons, and covered us in the shadow of death.
>
> He brought me up out of an horrible pit, the miry clay, and set my feet upon a rock, and established my goings.
>
> Deep calleth unto deep at the noise of thy waterspouts: all thy waves and thy billows are gone over me.

If I ascend up into heaven, thou art there: if I make my bed in hell, behold, thou art there. If I take the wings of the morning, and dwell in the uttermost parts of the sea: even there shall thy hand lead me, and thy right hand shall hold me.

And Job – Job he can hear:

For the thing which I greatly feared is come upon me, and that which I was afraid of is come unto me.

My days are past, my purposes are broken off, even the thought of my heart.

His confidence shall be rooted out of his tabernacle, and it shall bring him to the King of Terrors.

They came upon me as a wide breaking in of waters, in the desolation they rolled themselves upon me.

Hell is naked before me, and destruction hath no covering.

I am a brother to dragons and a companion to owls.

I have said to corruption, thou art my father: to the worm, thou art my mother and my sister.

Jonah he can hear

The waters compassed me about, even to the soul: the depth closed me round about, the weeds were wrapped about my head. I went to the bottoms of the mountains: the earth with her bars was about me forever: yet hast thou brought up my life from corruption, O Lord my God.

The cup of trembling he drinks.
The wine of astonishment he drinks.

And standing there alone on the Canyon floor, he breathes Kainozoic air, the same air that lizard and fox and egret and bighorn and humming bird and owl and moth and butterfly and squirrel and wood louse and rattlesnake breathe.

Sinking into himself, he breathes Mesozoic air, the same air that ichthyosaurus and tyrannosaurus and styracosaurus and ornithamimus and meganeura and mischoptera and archaeopteryx breathe.

And gone still further down into himself, gone down into his own embryonic origins, he 'breathes' Palaeozoic 'air', the same that sponge and jellyfish and crinoid and ammonite and trilobite and brachiopod breathe.

In him, as he stands there, the earth in all its geological ages is psychologically synchronous.

As crinoid he prays.

As styracosaurus he prays.

As bighorn he prays.
Little wonder that our myths of most nerve stop short.

Little wonder that our rituals of most nerve stop short.

Little wonder that Peter, James and John recoil and take refuge in sleep.

Little wonder that Nietzsche recoils and takes refuge with Somnus, in quotidian somnambulation.

But Jesus endures.

And, on a presumption of enabling grace, there is further evolution for us and for all things in watching with him.

And now, not red, and having a metaphorless look about it, Good Friday dawns upon us.
And our myths, even though it is only calamitously that they can comfort us, they have fallen behind.
And our stories and tall tales, even though it is only with happy or sad endings that they can comfort us, they too have fallen behind.
But, prompted by Christ himself in a dream, one of the Magi, the only one of them who is still alive, he has come back, and the wisdom-story he tells us pioneers a watching way for us:

No one in living memory had lived the religious life so intensely as Narada had. At an age when all the young men of his village had marriage in mind, he renounced the world and retired to a forest, practising austerities so damaging to life and limb they would soon have killed a lesser man. Over the years there was no obstruction, no matter how integral to his worldly identity, that he didn't take on. In the end, even Vishnu, the Great God himself, marvelled at his hunger and thirst, killing ordinary hunger and thirst, for final liberation and so it was that he did something he never before did. Coming down out of his high heaven, he stood in Narada's door, telling him that he would grant him any boon he desired. All he had to do was name it.

To know the secret of your Maya, Narada replied.
Vishnu smiled discouragingly.
Fierce in all his undertakings and ways, Narada persisted.
'Very well then', Vishnu said, 'we will walk together, you and I.

It was a long trudge through the forest and then, Vishnu complaining already of tiredness, they trudged through difficult scrubland.
They came into a red desert. So fierce was the sun, it didn't only boil their blood, it boiled their minds. Coming to a great rock and unable to put one buckling leg past the other, Vishnu sat down in its shallow shade, saying, 'here I stay, here I die, unless, of course, you find and bring me water, how soon you can see for yourself.'
Narada set off.
The only thing in him that didn't crack was his will.
He saw a green haze on the horizon.
And no, looking at it, he concluded that it wasn't a mirage. Indeed, now with every excited step of the way, it looked more real, and soon he was walking in the cool of great green trees.
He knocked on the first door he came to.

So instantly bewitched was he by the charm of the young woman who opened to him that he altogether forgot Vishnu in his distress. Utterly charmed, he walked in and sat down, neither he nor they of the house making strange with each other.

He ate an evening meal with them.
Next morning he went to work in their fields with them.
That's how it was for two whole years.
Alone with him one day, Narada asked the man of the house
for the hand of his daughter in marriage.
It was a joyous wedding.
A child, a boy, was born to them. Then a girl and again a girl.

Seven years later, the monsoon clouds were like oceans
hanging above the world and they hadn't far to fall and they all
seemed to fall together and within a few hours. Chaos swirling
and roaring everywhere, Narada and his family were out of
doors seeking the safety of higher ground. First one child,
then another was swept away. The old man and the old
woman were tumbled beneath a tumbling dyke. Then Narada
himself was engulfed and carried ten times down into ten ever
deeper drownings, only he didn't drown, couldn't drown, and
then, like waking from a dream or like waking from waking it
was, he was walking, his brain boiled, in a red desert, and all
around him, everywhere yet nowhere, he heard it, the voice of
the Great God asking, you've been gone for almost an hour,
did you bring the water ?

The question that would turn any day into Good Friday. Good Friday.
Dis-illusuioning day. Day we come to see that just as Narada walked into
the green haze so, having walked into it, are we bewitched by the world.
Only now, having undergone his dis-illusioning with Narada, we talk, not
about the world, but about the world-mirage, we talk about the world-illusion.

And what, we asked the Magus, what is the source of the world illusion?
How or where or in what does it arise ?
Judging us able for it, he tells us another story:

A man is walking home late one evening. Having worked all day under
the burning sun, he is looking forward to the cool of his house, to food
and rest. Suddenly he sees a snake, coiled and ready to strike, on the
side of the road. Reacting in terror, he leaps aside, aside and again
aside. At a safe distance, he opens his eyes and to his great relief he
sees, not a snake, but a coil of rope fallen most likely from an ox cart
trudging on ahead of him.

Out of our own minds the snake-illusion, the world-illusion, we say.

But, says the Magus, to know that is not yet to have won liberation. It isn't only Hindu traders who come to our land. Buddhist traders come, and a story they tell is our story too:

A prince by birth he was, a prince from a far away land, but after ten years with the world's greatest master in the arts of offence and defence he was called Prince Five Weapons, that in open recognition of his prowess in these same arts. Everyone sad to see him go, he set out for home. He came to a forest. People who lived within sight of it warned him saying, that if he valued his life he wouldn't so much as think of entering it because that, even that, would arouse the wrath of the ogre, called Sticky Hair, who lived in it.

Nothing daunted, Prince Five Weapons continued on his way, on and on, till he heard the roar that felled every tree between him and…whatever he was – a hundred shapes at once he was – and there he was, entertaining himself with his small-eyed rhinoceros charge and with his wide-horned, wide-nostrilled buffalo charge, with his invisible tiger stalk, with his open-jawed lion-leap into the tusked ogre, huge and sticky-haired, that he was during those very rare times when he could live with himself without having to endure the horror of being himself.

Sure of his aim, Prince Five Weapons launched his spear, it's head hungry for murder. For all the perfection of its flight, it shuddered and stopped dead in the Ogre's sticky hair.

Stretching a bow half as tall as himself, he released an arrow, it's head sleek with deadly venom. Reaching its target, it whirred and stopped dead, stuck in the sticky hair.

Closing upon him in a sequence of disconcerting sleights of movement, he struck with his sword. It stuck to him. Charging him with it, his dagger stuck to him. Bringing it down upon him, his club stuck to him. He hit him with his right fist. It stuck to him. He hit him with his left fist. It stuck to him. He pounded him with his head. It stuck to him. He kicked him with his right foot. It stuck to him. He kicked him with his left foot. It stuck to him.

What surprised and then enraged the Ogre was that even now, ripe though he was for devouring, Prince Five Weapons showed no fear. Why aren't you trembling? Sticky Hair raged. Why, like every one else who has dared to come this way, are you not pleading for your wretched little life ?

"Tis you should be trembling," Prince Five Weapons said. Shocked at first, the monster recovered and roared a buffalo roar, in huge, disbelieving derision.

"Roar as you will," said Prince Five Weapons, but not all of me is stuck to you, within me is eternal diamond life and if you swallow me it will shatter you as a thunderbolt would..

Astonished and fearing for himself, Sticky Hair trembled and, his devouring power over him at an end, Prince Five Weapons walked free.

Having given us a long time to reflect on how sticky the world might be and on how stuck to it we might be, it mattering but little whether that world be real or illusory, for to be stuck to a figment is as disabling as to be stuck to a fact – having given us Good Friday time to reflect on all of this, he told us that Prince Five Weapons was the Buddha in an earlier incarnation.

And he chanted for us the Buddha's Udana, the great and to us terrible words that he spoke on the morning of his enlightenment as he sat in the lotus position, touching the earth, requesting it to bear witness:

> Through many rounds
> From birth to death have I
> Toiled, seeking but not finding
> The builder of the house.
>
> House-builder, I behold you now;
> Again a house you will not build.
> All your rafters are broken now,
> The ridgepole also is thrown down:
> My mind, its elements dissolved,
> The end of craving has attained.

It is Good Friday, somewhere between the sixth and the ninth hour. It is like waking up, but not into waking. It is like waking up into dreamless sleep, into the no-thing-ness of dreamless sleep or into something beyond it that we have no name for.

Asking us to look up with our extinguished eyes and minds to the terrible summit, the Magus somehow gives us to know that it is to the crossed ridgepole and rafter of overthrown selfhood that Jesus is pinned back, and it is from here, his head falling forward onto his chest, that he looks down into the anasravic skull, his own and Adam's.

And now, still in baptismal assimilation to him, it remains to us to abide in the dark, it remains to us to be as out of God's way awake as we are in dreamless sleep.

And, down the centuries, many are they who have so abided, and many are they to whom God has been eternally gracious.

To Eckhart eternally gracious:

> Comes then the soul into the unclouded light of God. It is transported so far from creature-hood into nothingness that, of its own powers, it can never return to its agents or its former creaturehood. Once there, God shelters the soul's nothingness with his uncreated essence, safeguarding its creaturely existence. The soul has dared to become nothing, and cannot pass from its own being into nothingness and then back again, losing its own identity in the process, except God safeguarded it. This must needs be so.

> Oh, wonder of wonders, when I think of the union the soul has with God! He makes the enraptured soul to flee out of herself, for she is no more satisfied with anything that can be named. The spring of Divine Love flows out of the soul and draws her out of herself into the unnamed Being, into her first source, which is God alone.

To Marguerite Porete God was eternally gracious:

> Being completely free, and in command on her sea of peace, the soul is nonetheless drowned and loses herself through God, with him and in him. She loses her identity, as does the water from a river – like the Ouse or the Meuse – when it flows into the sea. It has done its work and can relax in the arms of the sea, and the same is true of the soul. Her work is over and she can lose herself in what she has totally become: Love. Love is the bridegroom of her happiness enveloping

her wholly in his love and making her part of that which is. This is a wonder to her and she has become a wonder. Love is her only delight and pleasure.

The soul now has no name but Union in Love. As the water that flows into the sea becomes sea, so does the soul become Love. Love and the soul are no longer two things but one. She is then ready for the next stage.

Reason: can there be a next stage after this?

Love: Yes, once she has become totally free, she then falls into a trance of nothingness, and this is the next highest stage. There she no longer lives in the life of grace, nor in the life of the spirit, but in the glorious life of divinity. God has conferred this special favour on her and nothing except his goodness can now touch her …What it means is being in God without being oneself, since to be in God is being…

To Henry Suso God was eternally gracious:

When the good and faithful servant enters into the joy of his Lord, he is inebriated by the riches of the house of God; for he feels, in an ineffable degree, that which is felt by the inebriated man. He forgets himself, he is no longer conscious of his selfhood; he disappears and loses himself in God, and becomes one spirit with him, as a drop of water which is drowned in a great quantity of wine. For even as such a drop disappears, taking the colour and taste of wine, so it is with those who are in full possession of blessedness…

Call it

Slí na Fírinne

Call it

The Adventure Of Our Immortality

As

Jesus Pioneered It

Call it

Jesus Crossing The Torrent

Into

Our Further and Final Evolution

In his letter to Ephesians St. Paul says that as well as ascending above all the heavens Jesus descended into the lowest parts of the Earth.

Let us imagine this descent.

In Arizona, in the American south-west, is the Grand Canyon.

Geologically immense in it's rockwalls and scree slopes and mesas and side-canyons, it is within itself a vast world two hundred and eighty miles long, four to eighteen miles wide from rim to rim and, descending through the accumulated sediments of thirteen ancient seafloors, it is a vertical mile deep. Under these seafloors, eating a yet deeper way for itself through rocks two thousand million years old, is the sometimes savagely cascading Colorado River, dropping ten thousand feet from source to sea. In a descending series from rim to river the old exposed sea beds, geological strata now, are called Kaibab, Toroweap, Coconino, Hermit, Supai, Redwall, Muav, Bright Angel, Tapeats, Shinumo, Hakatai, Bass and Vishnu. Starting well below the Mesozoic screeches of a pterosaur in featherless, bald-bodied flight, Bright Angel Trail takes us down through all thirteen sea beds, the deepest of them metamorphosed into dark schist, illuminated by intrusions of pink magma.

Not immediately companionable are magma and mind.

Not immediately companionable are Redwall and religion.

And yet, enforcing companionableness, we have named the mesas within the Canyon for goddesses and gods, themselves not at first sight companionable. At random, they are called the Vishnu Temple, the Brahma Temple, the Deva Temple, the Shiva Temple, Diana Temple, Vesta Temple and, cut down to human size, the Buddha Temple, the Zoroaster Temple, the Castor Temple, the Pollux Temple.

In the Canyon above all, ichthyosaurs swimming in seas two hundred million years above us and ammonites managing to move across seafloors two hundred million years beneath us, it surely isn't entirely wise to assume that nature will respond in kind to our naïve naming. Will Shiva, by residing in it, divinise the mesa we have reserved for him? Will Vishnu lighten the burden of matter to maya? Or, the next time we walk under a rockwall will we still imagine what would happen to us if it fell on us? Can maya hurt maya? And even if it can, there is on this understanding of things no reason to be upset, for the hurt itself is an illusion.

Quite obviously, religion colonized the eggs of a pterosaur at no cost to itself. Quite obviously, religion colonized the perfectly orthodonted mind of tyrannosaurus rex at no cost to itself.

Quite obviously, religion colonized the Canyon in all its rockwalls and falls at no cost to itself.

But, in the event that we believe that evolution is synonymous with moral improvement, there right before us is something that will give us pause, a living rattlesnake coiled about a fossilized trilobite, and that not just anywhere, that on Bright Angel shale.

The rattlesnake and Bright Angel.

What will Bright Angel think and do?

Will he think of the rattlesnake as everything that frustrates human wishes and will he do accordingly? Will he do what Marduk did? Marduk slew and sliced Tiamat, did it in a way that converted chaos to cosmos. Will he do what Atum the Egyptian Sungod did? Nightly in the underworld Atum decapitated Apophis, the terrible, bellowing snake-dragon sitting superlatively tall on his thousand coils. Will he do what Baal did? Thinking of Yam, the Abyss-Beast, as insatiably hostile to cosmos and culture, he rode out, he too, in his storm chariot and, as he so boastfully claimed, did successful final battle with him. Will he do what Yahweh did? Breaking the superbly insurgent seven heads of the Abyss-Beast, now called Rahab or Leviathan, Yahweh fed him to the flesh-famished peoples of the wilderness.

Given that divine precedent isn't wanting, what will Bright Angel do? Will he in his insecure hatred of him magnify rattlesnake to Tiamat size, to Apophis size, to Yam size, to Leviathan size? Will he turn dragon slayer? Will he, in effect, lobotomise earth and psyche, settling for lesser, less threatened, less frightened life? For tri-lobe-ite life? Or, ultimately, for lobeless life? For life unconscious of self and other-than-self. Or, at the very most, for life as we lived it in Babylon, Luxor, Jerusalem, Athens, Rome?

What are we to do?

Do we reproduce the Canyon as a Colosseum and say, here on summer afternoons, is fullness of civic-savage life?

Since, from the slaying of Tiamat till now, our world has been a Colosseum without walls, and since in consequence we are facing into ecological collapse, it would be sapient of us, would it not, to give ourselves a second chance with the Canyon?

Which, for reasons bearing yet more deeply on our condition, is what Jesus undertook and achieved.

As St. John the evangelist says, he crossed the Torrent.

As St. Paul says, he went down into the lowest parts of the Earth.

So it wasn't just the Kedron he crossed. Going all the way down to it, he crossed the Colorado, into our further and final evolution.

In the opening chapter of his Gospel, St. Mark has this to say about Jesus:

> And it came to pass in those days, that Jesus came from Nazareth of
> Galilee, and was baptized of John in Jordan. And straightway coming

up out of the water, he saw the heavens opened, and the Spirit like a
dove descending upon him: and there came a voice from heaven,
saying, Thou art my beloved Son, in whom I am well pleased. And
immediately the Spirit driveth him into the wilderness. And he was
there in the wilderness forty days, tempted of Satan; and was with the
wild beasts; and the angels ministered unto him.

Almost always it happens: no sooner the heavens opening above us than the
hell worlds opening beneath us, no sooner angels ministering to us than Satan
testing us.

And not only was Jesus with the wild beasts. Inwardly, out there in the
wilderness, he was with all that is beastly in us.

Not many nights would have passed when, like Job, he might have said, I am
a brother to dragons and a companion to owls.

Remembering the Psalm, he might have said, Thou hast sore broken me in the
place of dragons and covered me in the shadow of death.

Two nights later, again remembering, he might have said, Thou hast made me
to see hard things, Thou hast made me to drink the wine of astonishment.

Later that night, out there in the Judaean badlands, he might have said, Thou
hast made me to drink the dregs of the cup of trembling and wring them out.

A phrase of six words,

and was with the wild beasts

Properly read, short though it is, that phrase is two hundred and eighty miles
long, it varies from four to eighteen miles wide, from rim to river it is a vertical
mile deep.

And there is yet more.
What Jacob Boehme came to know, that Jesus endured:

In man is all what so ever the sun shines upon or heaven contains, also
hell and all the deeps.

What Sir Thomas Browne came to know, that he endured:

In our humanity we are a compendium of the six days, a cosmic
compendium.

What Joseph Conrad came to know, that he endured:

> The mind of man is capable of anything – because everything is in it, all the past as well as all the future.

Suffered before God and towards God, such plenary self-endurance is Passion and, to begin with Jesus had no choice in it, either to go towards it or to recoil from it:

the Spirit driveth him into the wilderness

Coming back from the wilderness in the power of the Spirit he overturned our world, with parables.

That done, this time by choice, a pterosaur flying fifty million years above him, he set out, down along Bright Angel Trail, down towards the Torrent thirteen and three quarters karmic miles below.

Divining what he had in mind, the gods and goddesses came to their temple doors and, knowing that what he was doing had never been imagined let alone undertaken, they did as much as they dared to do, they wished him well.

So passionately red were all rockwalls, it seemed that the Earth itself was willing him to do what he was doing.

Go down, Jesus

Go down, Jesus

Go down, Jesus

Go down into the lowest parts of the Earth, down below humanity, down below mammal, down below reptile, down below amphibian, down below fish, down below ammonite, down below alga, down below the first protein.

By the Torrent down there, in a depth where I is we, Bright Angel is waiting. He points to a rockpool that mirrors the thirteen and three quarters miles of stratified karma. Going down on his knees, Jesus cups his fin-fraught hands down into the water. When the water in this improvised chalice has settled and is again mirroring the karma of the ages he brings it to his lips and drinks it, to the lees, leaving nothing to wring out. All the while he has been doing this the Earth has been coming up over its own karmic horizon and there it is now

Gaiakhty

Next day, on the self-naughting Nunatak still within the Canyon, at a height where I is we, where the individual is cosmic compendium, he looked down into the universal empty skull and there it is now

Buddh Gaia

brightening the universe

Our creed is simple:

Jesus is the world's new story
All the way forward from its beginnings it is a

NEW WORLD

And the challenge to us is

INNOVATION

fully acknowledging that Jesus geologically endured the evolutionary
mutation of the Labyrinth into Bright Angel Trail,
fully acknowledging that Jesus has claimed the whole Canyon for culture, the
whole psyche for sanctity.

Call it

Slí na Fírinne

Call it

The Adventure Of Our Immortality

As

Jesus Pioneered It

Call it

Jesus Crossing The Torrent

Into

Our Further and Final Evolution

Call it

Watching With Jesus

Much as we might ask of a boat, is it seaworthy? so might we ask of the human psyche, is it worldworthy. More seriously, we must ask, is it selfworthy? Is it able for itself? Is it able for its own enormities? As Sir Thomas Browne might ask, is it able within itself to be a compendium of the six days? Is it able, relying only on what it is in itself, to be consciously a compendium of the six days? And, on the assumption that it is in fact a compendium of the six days, across how much of it and down into how much of it does the ego's jurisdictive writ run?

We can guess, given what he knew, what Jacob Boehme's answer would be:

> In man is all whatsoever the sun shines upon
> or heaven contains, also hell and all the deeps.

We can guess, given what he knew, what Gerard Manley Hopkins' answer would be:

> O the mind, mind has mountains, cliffs of fall
> Frightful, sheer, no-man-fathomed. Hold them cheap
> May who ne'er hung there …

We can guess, given what he knew, what Joseph Conrad's answer would be:

> The mind of man is capable of anything – because everything is in it,
> all the past as well as all the future.

We can guess what, in their phylogenetic engulfment, Pasiphae, Andromeda, Hippolytus, Actaeon and Oedipus would say.

Permanent and complete engulfment such as Coatlicue underwent is one of the risks we run when we cross the Torrent with Jesus.

Should we therefore not so much as think of crossing it with him?

The truth is, given how we are constituted, we are at risk irrespective of where we are, idling here or seeking there, as little aware as we can be on this side of the Torrent or fully aware on the far side of it.

What to do?

Do we do what Peter, James and John did? Do we take refuge in sleep?

Then cometh Jesus with them unto a place called Gethsemane, and saith unto the disciples, sit ye here, while I go and pray yonder. And he took with him Peter and the two sons of Zebedee, and began to be sorrowful and very heavy. Then saith he unto them, my soul is exceeding sorrowful, even unto death: tarry ye here, and watch with me. And he went a little further, and fell on his face, and prayed, saying, O my Father, if it be possible, let this cup pass from me: nevertheless not as I will but as thou wilt. And he cometh unto the disciples, and findeth them asleep, and saith unto Peter, what, could ye not watch with me one hour? Watch and pray, that ye enter not into temptation: the spirit indeed is willing, but the flesh is weak. He went away again the second time, and prayed, saying, O my Father, if this cup may not pass away from me, except I drink it, thy will be done. And he came and found them asleep again: for their eyes were heavy. And he left them and went away again, and prayed the third time, saying the same words. Then cometh he to his disciples, and saith unto them, sleep on now, and take your rest: behold, the hour is at hand…

Imperilled by a double discovery, Nietzsche took refuge in sleep:

I have discovered for myself that the old human and animal life, indeed the entire pre-history and past of all sentient being, works on, loves on, hates on, thinks on, in me.

I suddenly woke up in the midst of this dream, but only to the consciousness that I am dreaming and that I must go on dreaming lest I perish – as a somnambulist must go on dreaming lest he fall.

Jesus chose precisely otherwise. Crossing into Gethsemane, he chose to awaken to all that we phylogenetically and extraphylogenetically are. Climbing to the place or summit of the skull, he chose to wake up from waking.

In the light of this, how solitarily awe-ful are his words:

sleep on now

As for us, there are good reasons to choose as Nietzsche chose and there are good reasons to choose as Narada chose.

Vishnu's gentle stay on his eagerness notwithstanding, Narada would awaken.

And to some of us, if not yet to all of us, Christ's invitation remains:

tarry ye here, and watch with me

And St. Paul sees our baptism not just as an invitation to watch, he sees it as an invitation to undergo:

> Know ye not, that so many of us as were baptized into Jesus Christ were baptized into his death? Therefore we are buried with him by baptism into death: that like as Christ was raised up from the dead by the glory of the Father, even so we also should walk in newness of life.

To Romans he says,

> now it is high time to awake out of sleep

Extending its meaning mystically, this we can understand to be saying,

> now it is high time to do what Jesus did

> now it is high time to look down into the empty skull

> now it is high time to walk back through the rent in dualizing consciousness as it deludes us asleep and awake.

The question remains: how seaworthy is the human psyche? We only have to remember how suddenly it opened at the seams in Job and Jonah:
> When I say my bed shall comfort me, my couch shall ease my complaint, then thou scarest me with dreams and terrifiest me through visions, so that my soul chooseth strangling and death rather than my life.

> The waters compassed me about, even to the soul: the depth closed me round about, the weeds were wrapped about my head. I went down to the bottoms of the mountains: the earth with her bars was about me for ever …

Push not off, is Ishmael's advice.
And yet how can we live with the three most terrible words ever addressed to us

> sleep on now

Nietzsche and Narada.
Nietzsche's choice as perilous perhaps as Narada's.
What to do?

That the Earth is an evolutionary success all the way forward from its beginnings is an opportunity for us to be other than how we have been. Indeed, if the Earth is to continue brightening our corner of the universe we must be other than how we have been.

Starting from the lowest parts of the Earth, Jesus pioneered a trail all the way back to the Divine Source. He pioneered it for all things, for stegosaurus and rhinoceros as well as for mollusc and Moses.

In the interest of our further and final evolution we need to select this trail. As nature selects a favourable mutation we need to select it. Suggesting enormities, we need to select it as nature has selected metamorphosis in insects. Not that the trail is a matter merely of trans-form-ation, of transition from one to another form. It is something fearfully and marvellously more.

The best way or maybe the only way to select the trail is to reconfigure it into ritual, into legomena and dromena, into sacred things sacredly said, into sacred things sacredly done.

Fortunately, we already have a ritual which, with some adjustments, meets our need. We have

Tenebrae

The name is variously derived from the canonical accounts of Christ's Passion, St. Luke's for instance, in Latin:

Erat autem fere hora sexta, et tenebrae factae
sunt in universam terram usque in horam nonam.
Et obscuratus est sol: et velum templi scissum est medium…

And it was about the sixth hour, and there was a darkness
over all the earth until the ninth hour. And the sun was darkened,
and the veil of the temple was rent in the middle…

As it was traditionally performed, Tenebrae was the ritual in which we watched with Jesus from the moment he crossed the Torrent until, on the third day following, he reappeared in the Garden of the Sepulchre.

Briefly, this is how it was enacted.

A candelabrum, called the Tenebrae harrow or the Tenebrae hearse, was carried in and set upon a standard in the sanctuary. Triangular in shape, it had seven candles on each ascending side and, making fifteen in all, a candle at the apex.

Sitting cowled in their choir stalls, the fully lighted harrow between them, the monks gave solemn and unhurried Gregorian voice to Christ entering upon his Passion. This they did chanting antiphons drawn from the great tragic psalms. A cantor chanted an entire Passion narrative. Building to a sense of final destructive desolation and abandonment, the Lamentations of Jeremiah were chanted. Concurrently with all of this, at prescribed intervals, a candle would be quenched. Finally, only the candle at the apex was still lighting and this was now taken down and taken round behind the altar and entombed there, leaving the church in darkness. So it was that we shook off sleep and watched with Jesus passionately pioneering a trail for all things. So it was that we passionately accompanied him all the way. So it was that we pioneered with him into the darkness of Good Friday. So it was that we abided in

Tenebrae

until, blazing upon us, the light of Easter would have utterly comprehended us inward and downward to the core and root of our brightening lives.

A great ritual. The greatest that humanity is heir to.

A ritual demiurgic to a new humanity.

A ritual that promotes us into and through our further and final evolution

Imagine it.

In baptismal assimilation to Jesus, he doing it for us, we cup our hands down into the mirroring rockpool on the floor of the Karmic Canyon. Next day, still within the Canyon, he doing it for us, we look down into the empty skull.

In this we very obviously aren't humanists relying entirely on our own resources. On the contrary. Always aware of how unseaworthy within itself the human psyche is, we at all times lay and hold ourselves radically open to Divine assistance. Indeed, given how inwardly precipitous we are, as in Pasiphae, Actaeon, Oedipus, we must be careful, especially on the far side of the Torrent, to not ask too much of ourselves and, above all, to not be over bold. Some there are who to their cost will have learned that every ladder continues gapingly downwards as a labyrinth and for that reason alone we have need of nothing less than the greatest of rituals, we have need of

Tenebrae

Imagine it, a seven branched, or better
a nine branched harrow

It is our senses and faculties that we quench on the way into

       the cloud of unknowing

on the way into

       the dark night of the soul

on the way into

       Tenebrae

Imagine it.
The Grail Quest accomplished, we set out on a new quest, the Tenebrae Quest, a quest to script and score a ritual which, being a way through, will see us through to blessedness in

       God

to blessedness in

       Buddh Gaia

JUBILATIONS

.

Sounding now and always

are the

Four Trumpet Blasts

are the

Four Jubilations

that announce a new world.

I

How beautiful upon the Mountains of Ararat are the feet of him who comes to announce that

a child is born unto us

II

As the Gospels see him, Jesus is eminent in miracle, parable and passion.

Miracle:

When the temperature drops to freezing point, strange and unexpected things happen. Moisture in the air marvels to snowflakes. Turbulent streams are hung up in rock-like silence, in ice. As though they had become a silver dream of themselves, trees, and none more beautifully than birch trees, bloom all over with hoar frost.

Much as there is freezing point in nature so is there a miracling point in it. Indeed, for those who have eyes to see, nature is always and everywhere a miracling.

Some there are who, sinking down into it, live from miracling nature and so it is that Jesus only has to walk past it and the dead tree blooms.

Parable:

Coming back into it after forty days in the wilderness, Jesus overturned our much too worldly world, with five parables.

Passion:

No small matter to have suffered the Earth in all its geological ages. No small matter to have suffered it to evolutionary success.

III

What Jesus undertook to do and did in the Karmic Canyon is an event so new and so vast under the sun, that the sun itself and the stars are Earth-brightened.

And that alters the old astrological order, influences from now on flowing out upon the stars from the Earth as well as in upon the Earth from the stars.

IV

It isn't primarily with our intelligence that we brighten our galaxy. It is in practicing nirvikalpasamadhi that we do so.

Nirvikalpasamadhi is a Sanskrit word. It signifies a state of non-dualizing consciousness.

That there are among us some who attain to nirvikalpasamadhi and some who attain to reimersion beyond being and non-being in God, that is the bright but supraspectral distinction of our hundred million local stars.

Here, in Slí na Fírinne, our confidence in ourselves as Christians enables us, no matter what it's provenance, to listen to the wisdom of humanity. While we do not relapse into polytheistic credence in doing so, we listen to a Bhagavad Gita sung to us at sea by the god of the sea. In it he challanges us to come out of the prison-house of common perception into silver branch perception or, as a Christian would name it, Paradisal perception.

In challenging us to emerge into silver branch perception he is challenging us to emerge into silver branch morality, into silver branch behaviour towards all things.

A BHAGAVAD GITA SUNG TO US AT SEA
BY
THE GOD OF THE SEA

Great and renowned warrior that he was, it wasn't something that Bran Mac Feabhail had ever done, but one day, drawn to he didn't know what, he walked out of his fortress, down and away into the wet, wild lands where only snipe and herons and otters lived. Before long, he having always been a man among men, the silence and the solitude were getting to him. A red onslaught between mountains, that he could deal with, but this silence that you couldn't spear, this solitude that you couldn't bring a sword down upon, even the mist that came down, it all unnerved him. Suffering his first defeat, he turned for home. Soon, his walking a trudging, he heard music not of our world behind him. Turning round, he saw a silver branch. It was out of it the music came. Strangest of all, the branch didn't play it. What he heard was the branch being itself. Being itself, it had perils for mortals in it. And it raided him. In the way that he himself would raid a triple-ditched ringfort, it raided him. It raided him, not with spear and torch and sword, with its unearthly sweetness it raided him. Almost, almost to swooning. Then it ceased, and, by the time he came back to himself and opened his eyes, it was gone.

In his hall that night, amidst all the usual goings on, Bran sat silent and alone. A hard man in battle and in all his dealings with the world, it had never occurred to him that anything either in the world or from beyond it could have so disabled him.

Whatever else, the music had damaged him in his sense of himself.
And his people – when they came to know, it would damage him in their eyes.
He imagined their great concern. Bran Mac Feabhail, the hard man, not foremost in battle. Bran Mac Feabhail, his eyes and his mind not fixed on what he was doing. Bran Mac Feabhail laid low not by a sword stroke but by longing.
Sensing a sudden silence in the house, he opened his eyes and there she was, a radiant woman, cruel if she needed to be.

Fifty quatrains she sang, singing of the wonders of the land she came from. And he, Bran, him she invited to come to that land.
Next morning, in three ships, in each ship a company of three times nine men, he was on the sea, sailing westward.
After two days and two nights of tough, untoward going, suddenly, instead of sea salt in their eyes and minds, the fragrances, blent and separate, of summer meadows, and there he was, Manannan Mac Lir, god of the sea, riding towards them in his four horse chariot. Singing them out over the manes and heads of his

horses, they still trampling, thirty quatrains he sang:

Cáini amra laisin mBran
ina churchán tar muir nglan;
          os mé, am charput do chéin,
          is magh sccothach ima-réidh.

A n-us muir glan
don náoi broindig a tá Bran,
          is Mag Meall co n-iumat scoth
          damsa a carput dá roth.

At-chí Bran
lín tonn tibri tar muir nglan.
          At-chíu ca-déin i mMagh Mon
          sgotha cennderga gin on.

Taithnit gabra lir a sam
sella roiscc ro sire Bran.
          Brunditt sscotha sruaim do mil
          a crích Manannáin mic Lir.

Lí na fairge fora taí,
geldod mora imme-roí:
          ra sert buidhe ocus glas;
          is talam nád écomrass.

Lingit ích bricc ass de brú,
a muir finn forn-aiccisiu;
          it láoig it uain co ndath,
          co cairde, cin imarbad.

Cé at-chetha áonchairptheach
i mMag Meall co n-immat scoth,
          fil mor di echaib ar brú
          cen suide, nát aiccisiu ……

    The god telling us how different is the world as he sees it from the world as we see it.

    The god telling us that what we, rising and falling in it, see as grey, salt sea, he sees as a Plain of Delights over which, even now, he is riding in his four-horse chariot.

The god telling us that, if only we had eyes to see, we would see that the silver branch being itself is no more wonderful than any ordinary ash branch or oak branch being itself.

And what the god doesn't tell us in words he tells us in his singing. His singing being the singing of the silver branch, he tells us that, had we eyes to see it, any ordinary bush being itself would put an end to us being our everyday selves.

Signalling to his men to turn their boats round, Bran sailed home to the land he had left, the land to which the radiant lady had invited him. Waiting for him there on the shore, the silver branch sang the song of his ascent into Ireland.

Over months and then over years it would happen. Bran would be out on his own in the wetlands or he'd be on his way home, alone, from an assembly of his people and, full in front of him on an otter trail or on a chariot road, there it would be, the silver branch singing six other stanzas that Manannán sang at sea:

> Sech is Manannán mac Lir
> asin charput cruth in fir,
>> bied dia chlaind densa ngair
>> fer cáoin hi curp criad adgil.

> Con-lee Manannán mac Lir
> luth lighe la Caointigirn:
>> gerthair dia mach i mbith gnó;
>> ad-ndidma Fiachna mac ndó.

> Moidfid sognáis gach sidhe;
> bid treitil cach daghthíre;
>> at-fii rúna rith ecne
>> isin mbith can a ecli.

> Bieid hi fethol cech míl
> itir glasmuir ocus tír;
>> bid druac re mbuidnib hi froiss;
>> bid cú allaid cech indroiss.

> Bid dam co mbennuiph argait
> hi mruig I nd-agthar carpait;
>> bid écni brec, i llinn lain;

bid rón, bid eala fionbán.

Biaid tre bitha síora
Cét mbliadna hi findrighe;
    silis learca lecht imchían;
    dergfaid roí roth imrían.

Manannán, god of the sea, telling us at sea, or what to us is sea, that he will come ashore into Ireland, that he will lie with a woman called Caointigirn, that a son she and her husband will call Mongán mac Fiachna will be born to her, that he will be welcome in all worlds, that he will be both seer and sage, that sometimes when he talks it will seem like it is the oldest bush in Ireland that is talking. Other times, listening to him, it will seem like you are surrounded by an oakwood and that it is telling you the deepest common secret of its being and your own being. Perfectly human when he is human, he will not nonetheless be so perfectly held as so many of us are to the habit of being human. When he needs to, he will be a dragon. Not content to know the world in only a human way, he will be seal, he will be swan. Challenging us in our miserable habits of seeing and knowing, he will walk towards us as a silver antlered stag. A king in the land, he will put down evil but in doing so he will not himself become evil.
Even people who know him only be hearsay will know, hearing about him, that Mongán Mac Fiachna is a Son of God.
Son of the most tremendous of gods, Manannán Mac Lir, god of the sea, of what to us is sea, of what to him is a plain of delights.

Never are we so challenged in all that we are as we are when we encounter Manannán.
The instant we meet him we know that eye and mind are habits of eye and mind.
The instant we meet him we know that the world we have lived in was all along but a habit of seeing, a habit of knowing.
The instant we meet him we know that being human is a habit and, walking away, we know how shaken in that habit we now are.
And how glad we are to be so shaken in this habit of being human, shaken in it and, at times, shaken altogether out of it.
To be human, when being human is a habit we have broken, that is a wonder.
And when, as will happen, we take being human for granted, how good it then is to walk out of it and be a seal in the sea off Tory or a swan on Lough Deirg Deirc.

But, having been out of our humanity for days or months or years, there is no wonder so great as the wonder of coming back into it.

The outlandish danger and difficulty of it, that is the wonder of coming back into it, of being in it.

No wonder we so yearningly call upon it to come and condense all about us. What a wonder and a blessing it is to a naked spirit when a human body begins to condense all about it, when human hearing, seeing, touch, taste and smell condense all about it, when human seeking and knowing condense all about it. Here it is, again setting out on the most perilous of adventures, the adventure of being what we are, human beings for whom their humanity is a conscious choice.

All of this was Bran Mac Feabhail's answering song to the Song of God he heard at sea.

Calling for silence, he sang it in his house.

Calling for silence, he sang it at assemblies of his people.

Calling for silence, he sang it at fairs all over the country.

Not needing to call for silence, he sang it to otters and herons and snipe in the wetlands.

This was Bran preparing Ireland for the day when Manannán would come ashore into Ireland.

It's what Ireland means, Bran one day said to his druid.

What, his druid asked, does Ireland mean?

It means what Manannán singing at sea means.

Simply it means

Silver branch perception of things in their silver branch being.

Then Ireland isn't for living in, the druid said.

How so? Bran asked.

How if I see it in its silver branch being, how if I hear it in its silver branch singing in root and branch, can I cut down a tree and make a chariot of it? How it I see it in its silver branch being, how if I hear it in its silver branch lowing, can I kill a yearling calf and eat it?

A calf out at grass is silver branch being, Bran said. A calf slaughtered outside in our yard is silver branch being, is silver branch singing, in hoof and horn. A beef hanging from a cross beam here in our house is silver branch being, is silver branch singing, in hough and split chest. Whatever its condition or state, being is silver branch being. But yes, you are right, altered perception must mean and will mean altered behaviour.

The sea being what it is in his perception of it doesn't deter Manannán from riding over it in a four horse chariot, the druid said.
So?
So we might as well live in the world as it used to be.
To talk about the world as it used to be is to talk about our eyes and minds as they used to be, Bran said.

Manannán did come ashore.

Sometimes people who lived far away from people would see him, a silver antlered stag walking alone.

But of all the people who lived in Ireland at that time only Bran was willing to pay the price of conversion to silver branch seeing and knowing.

And that to this day is what Ireland is.

Less and less as time goes by do the people who live in it know that Ireland is Manannán lost cause.

Are you content that this is so?

Looking back at it from the Moon or from Mars, are you content that our planet is Manannán's lost cause?

Here at home, standing before a bush in Cnoc an Utha, can you be content with anything less than the mirum and the morality of Manannán's

At-chíu

OUR BHAGAVAD GITA

A CHRISTIAN TRANSLATION

Having heard that Bran Mac Feabhail had met Manannán Mac Lir, god of the sea, out at sea, St. Patrick turned in at his gate or, as it turned out, at the three sequent gates of his triple-ditched ringfort, each ditch perfectly palisaded and, as though he was expected, torches lighted at all three sets of gate posts.
And yes, Bran did look like someone who had seen God. Even as he looked at you, his eyes fully on you, he was still looking seaward.
What Manannán had said to Bran, singing it out over the manes and heads of his chariot horses at sea, that is what everyone Patrick had met walking west along the road had talked about, warrior and druid and child and crone and swineherd and cattle-reaver and seeress singing it:

> Cáini amra laisin mBran
> ina churchán tar muir nglan;
>   os mé, am charput do chéin
>   is magh sccothach ima-réidh.

> A n-us muir glan
> don náoi broindig a tá Bran,
>   is Mag Meall co n-iumat scoth
>   damsa a carput dá roth.

> At-chí Bran
> lín tonn tibri tar muir nglan.
>   At-chíu ca-déin i mMagh Mon
>   sgotha cennderga gin on

> Taithnit gabra lir a sam
> sella roiscc ro sire Bran.
>   Brundit sscotha sruaim do mil
>   a crích Manannáin mic Lir.

> Lí na fairge fora taí
> geldod mora imme-roí:
>   ra sert buidhe ocus glas

is talam nád écomrass.

Lingit ich bricc ass de brú
a muir finn forn-aiccisiu;
    it láoig it úain co ndath,
    co cairde, cin imarbad …

Manannán, a god, telling Bran, a mortal, what to you is bitter sea is to me a plain of delights, what to you is an endless, aimless heaving this way and that is to me a perfect world, nothing in it that isn't as perfect as an otter's face or as the fragrance of a primrose.

All of this Patrick knew, having heard it so often in so many local accents as it spread across the country, turning off chariot roads onto cow tracks, onto paths through woods and to wells and from wells to every house for miles about.

Why? Patrick asked a man he heard singing it at a fair. Why do sing it over and over and over again?

Because it is what it is, that's why I sing it, he said. I sing it because it is a Song of God, and while I'm singing it here at the centre, be sure that it is also being sung at the four corners of Ireland. For the first time ever all royal and tribal boundaries have gone down in Ireland. For the first time ever Ireland is one. It is one in a sung song of God.

And again, crowds around him, he began:

Cáini amra laisin mBran
ina churchán tar muir nglan;
    os mé, am charput do chéin
    is magh sccothach ima-réidh.

What Patrick wasn't at all sure of, even though he had heard so much about it, was the silver branch. What had it to do with all of this? When and how did it first appear? Its music, could anyone endure it? Was it still among us? Had it come to stay? And if it had, what would that mean? A totally new way of understanding ordinary things? A totally new way, or perhaps a dangerously new way, of relating to river and star? The silver branch among us? Was that Manannán's way of seeing things among us? Is reality our way of seeing it or Manannán's way of seeing it? And if it is as Manannán sees it how can we ever pick it off a briar to feed ourselves, how can we ever chop it to warm ourselves, how when we need to piss can we so far dare as to actually piss on it? Or is it that the singing of the silver branch is in our pissing too? Is our pissing a Song of God? The Song of God the man sang at the fair?

A n-us muir glan
Don náoi broindig a tá Bran,
      is Mag Meall co n-iumat scoth
      damsa a carput dá roth …

Is this the Pagan Gospel?
Patrick needed to know and that was why, night falling on him, that he walked through all three torch-lit gates and, sitting in front of him, put these two questions to Bran: how perfect is an otter's face when he has a brown trout between his teeth? what does the trout think?
A strange thing happened to me one day, Bran said. For the first time in my life I felt a big inconvenient need to be on my own, and silence, I wanted to know what that was like. At the cost of my people thinking that something bad was happening to me, I walked out and down and away into the wetlands, and yes, there was silence there, and solitude, more of both of them that I felt I could take. It was hard on me. Anything I could hurl a spear at or take a sword to I could deal with, but how having beaten it back, how having cornered it, could I shove a sword in solitude. For the first time in my long warrior's life I knew defeat. 'Twas as if, cupping my hand down into it, I had drunk defeat. Me? Me defeated? Me defeated, not be Ferdia, but by solitude? Me defeated, not by Cuchulainn, but by silence? Would they see it in me? My people, would they see that I had been defeated, it making no difference by what? And what then of their continuing willingness to be led by me, to be ruled by me? Where normally I'd have turned for home I turned to day to come back and face insurgency. Then, listening downheartedly to the plashing of my feet in water as I walked, I heard it, a music surely not of our world. Even my bones, even my mind. I thought it would melt. Turning round, I saw a silver branch, and it wasn't that it was making the music as a singer or as a harper might. It was the music. In its very being it was the music. It threatened me in all that I was. Not laying a hand on me, it raided me. Listening to it, if what I was doing was listening to it, I died to all habits of eye and mind in me. Listening to it, for a moment, only for a moment, I mattered as little to me as I do every night in dreamless sleep. Not because it had mercy on me, it ceased. Eventually, enough of who and what I used to be came back to me, and I walked home.

Caring not at all what druid or warrior or poet or harper or smith might think, I sat in silence that night, our usual bright life going on all around me.
Suddenly, in the middle of loud but good-humoured uproar there was silence. Withdrawing my hand from before my eyes, I saw a woman surely not of our world and what startled me was that her singing was the singing of the silver

branch. Having no care for us, having no mercy on us, fifty quatrains she sang celebrating the world she came from and, the thing seeming like a doom to me, she invited me, or was it that she commanded me, to come and live in it.

Next morning, a company of three times nine warriors in each of three ships, we put out to sea, a spitting, wet wind of two minds where it wanted to blow from making life hard for us. After a day and a night our hands felt pickled. By evening it was our eyes, and soon, the way things were going, it would be our minds.

We toiled all night and, every ship's length of headway hard to hold on to, we toiled all morning, and then, hearing the thunder of him coming, we saw him, Manannán Mac Lir, god of the sea, coming over the sea.

Out over the manes and heads of his chariot horses he sang, Manannán singing to us, or, you could say, it was the silver branch singing to us, or, yet again, you could say that it was reality itself that was singing to us, telling us that it isn't as we perceive it:

> At-chí Bran
> Lín tonn tibri tar muir nglan.
> > at-chiú ca-déin i mMagh Mon
> > sgotha cennderga gin on.

And what surprised us all the more, and frightened us all the more, was this: still singing to us out over the manes and heads of his thunder horses, Manannán, god of the sea, telling us that he will soon come ashore into Ireland, not to appear to us, but to lie with a woman called Caointigirn. As he sang of him, his singing the singing of the silver branch, we could see him, the Son of God who would be born among us, who would walk among us:

> Moidfid sognáis gach sídhe;
> bid treitil cach daghthíre;
> > at-fii rúna rith ecne
> > isin mbith can a ecli

> Bieid hi fethol cech míl
> itir glasmuir ocus tír;
> > bid druac re mbuidnib hi froiss;
> > bid cú allaid cech indroiss.

> Bid damh co mbennuiph argait
> hi mruig i nd-agthar carpait;

bid écni brec i llinn lain;
bid rón, bid eala fionnbán.

Biaid tre bitha síora
cét mbliadna hi findrighe;
silis learca lecht imchían,
dergfaid roí roth imrían ...

He will be welcome in all worlds and in all dimensions of any one world. To all mysteries and secrets he will have answers. When he needs to, he will be a dragon, he will be a wolf. Not limiting himself to one way, to one way only, of experiencing himself and the world, he will be a speckled salmon in a pool that mirrors mountains. The sea calling him, he will be a seal. A swan in a lake alone he will be. Seeing a silver-antlered stag walking to a river to drink, a swineherd will say to his fellow, that's him, that's the Son of God. Riding into it in a jewelled, four-horse chariot, he will redden a battlefield, fighting evil. Not just for thirty or sixty or seventy years will he live among us. No tree sown on the year of his birth will outlast him. People will think of him as they do of rivers and mountains, always with us.

Having heard as much as I was able to hear about reality and about our life with the silver-antlered Son of God, I commanded their captains to turn our ships round.

An emanation of reality as it is, the silver branch ascended the shingles into Ireland with us.

It was to the land we had always lived in that the woman, one of our own, had invited us.

In every ordinary branch, whether oak branch or ash branch, is the singing of the silver branch.

Just as well that I didn't know that day that I was setting out on the most difficult of voyages, that the voyage to where we are.

More terrible than wonderful it is that our

Song of God

is about ourselves and our world, about our eyes and everything they see, about the holes in the sides of our heads and everything they hear, about our hands and everything we in our greed grab.

This voyage to where we are, it's what everyone all over Ireland is talking about, Patrick said. And they aren't only talking about it. Either they are turning their ships and their lives around or, the silver branch coming up the shingle shore before them, they are coming home to where they already are. It's to a state of eye and mind they are coming home. And ask anyone anywhere in Ireland now to sing a song and its our

Song of God

is about ourselves and our world, about our eyes and everything they see, about the holes in the sides of our heads and everything they hear, about our hands and everything we in our greed grab.

This voyage to where we are, it's what everyone all over Ireland is talking about, Patrick said. And they aren't only talking about it. Either they are turning their ships and their lives around or, the silver branch coming up the shingle shore before them, they are coming home to where they already are. It's to a state of eye and mind they are coming home. And ask anyone anywhere in Ireland now to sing a song and its our

Song of God

they will sing.

Ireland, for now, is a voyage, it is a Bran's voyage to where we are. Indeed a man I met on the road welcomed me not to Ireland but to

BRAN'S VOYAGE TO WHERE WE ARE

It is what they are calling Ireland now, they are calling it

Imram Brain

You are welcome, he said, to silver branch seeing and to silver branch knowing. And you are welcome, he said, to settle here. To settle here, he added, in the delighting knowledge that the Silver Antlered Son of God is with us, is one of us. And it isn't only us who can say that. Seals say it. Wolves say it. Swans say it. Deer say it. Dragons say it. Singing it in every branch, trees say it. The shingles of the shore you climbed coming here say it.
And you, Bran asked, do you say it.
It will delight me, as it now so obviously delights everyone, when I am able to

say it, Patrick said.

There is a question I would ask you, Patrick said.

Ask it, Bran said.

What do you do when you need to piss?

I go out and I piss.

With no sense of sacrilege against the singing of the silver branch in the grass you piss on?

The singing of the silver branch isn't in one thing and not in another, Bran said. It is in everything, even in the cancer that is killing me.

Now, the full moon lighting my way, I go north, Patrick said.

North to where? Bran asked.

North to a scatter of people who live near Foclut Wood.

And what, might I ask, is your business with them?

I will talk to them about the Son of God who knows what it is to be a brown trout in an otter's mouth.

Then there is a further question I would ask you, Bran said.

Ask it, Patrick said.

That scatter of people who live near Foclut Wood – will you sing Manannán's song to them? Will you induct them into silver branch seeing and knowing?

More likely, Patrick said, that they will induct me, challenging me as Christ does to consider the lily of the field, the twig on my path.

So why are you a Christian?

I have told you, haven't I?

Tell me again.

The coincidence of silver branch ontology and savagery in an otter's teeth, in my own teeth.

If the world is what Keats says it is, a vale of soul-making, then time spent in once-upon-a-time isn't time misspent.

COMING OUT OF THE ANAESTHETIC
(Coming in to plenitude of being in the plenary world)

Talking with her recently, my niece Amanda reminded me that humanity has in the past been afflicted by some very destructive diseases, among them plague, pox and tuberculosis. The next big disease, she feared, will be madness.

In what sense madness? I enquired.

Madness in the sense of mental alienation from our deep mind and from how reality is, she replied.

Afterwards, sitting on alone, I wondered what she meant by our deep mind.

I remembered something Yeats said:

I know now that revelation is from the self, but from that age-long memoried self, that shapes the elaborate shell of the mollusc and the child in the womb, that teaches the birds to make their nests; and that genius is a crisis that joins that buried self for certain moments to our trivial daily mind.

I remembered something a remembering Inuit said:

In the very earliest time when both people and animals lived on earth a person could become an animal if he wanted to and an animal could become a human being. Sometimes they were people and sometimes animals, and there was no difference. All spoke the same language. That was the time when words were like magic. The human mind had mysterious powers. A word spoken by chance might have strange consequences. It would suddenly come alive and what people wanted to happen could happen – all you had to do was say it. Nobody can explain this: that's the way it was.

It is of things as they now are that J.B.S. Haldane speaks when he says:

It is my suspicion that the universe isn't only queerer than we suppose, it is queerer than we can suppose.

On the assumption that this is so, it must be good for us, it might even reconnect us with how reality is, were we to spend some time in Once-Upon-a-Time.

Once upon a time a hunter lived by himself in a lonely place, lonely even for

48

owls. Every morning at first light he would leave his hut and set out on a great round checking his snares and nets and traps. Coming home one evening with only a hare hanging from his belt, it surprised him and frightened him to see smoke rising from his chimney. How can it be? he wondered. In a world where he never saw any human footprints but his own? All his senses alert, he pushed open the door, only to see that as well as a great blazing fire on the hearth there was a steaming hot meal on the table. Not sure that it was the right thing to do, he sat down and ate the food and then, not daring to take the tongs to it, he sat by the fire, wondering. Now to night his house was no longer a refuge from the world. The strangeness and danger and wonder of the world had come indoors. It steamed from his table. It blazed from his hearth. Would he ever again, he wondered, be able to come in out of the world and close his door on it? Would he ever again be able to come in out of the world and close his hunter's mind on it?

Next morning, again at first light, he was on his way. That evening, careful to stay downwind from a boar and her litter, he turned for home and, from a long way off, he saw it, smoke rising from his chimney. His hunter's senses alert, walking as silently as his shadow, he reached his door and, as though anything could happen, he opened it, wincing when it creaked. As he expected it would be, the strangeness and danger and wonder of the world was in his house, blazing from his hearth, steaming from his table.

To night again he ate the danger. Fearing that it might spring at him, he sat beside it, flaming on the hearth.

Next morning, his curiosity overcoming a sense of respect, he turned off his track and, sitting concealed in a clump of bushes, he kept his house in view. It wasn't long till he saw a fox trotting all the way to his door and pushing it open. Soon there was smoke from his chimney, and so, instead of continuing on his round, he retraced his steps, walking now again as noiselessly as his shadow. As much as with a deep, slow breath as with his hand, he opened the door. He saw a woman hanging a pot over the fire and as he closed it he saw a fox pelt hanging from a peg on the back of his door.

A woman who was a fox or a fox who had become a woman, he knew that she was aware of him, but she didn't acknowledge him.

Not yet.

Not yet.

Not yet.

In the end, looking at him only for as long as it took her to say it, she said, I have come to live with you.

It was a new life for the hunter.

Every morning he had dry, well-mended clothes to put on.

Every evening, from a long way off, he'd see smoke from his chimney.

It was, though, a difficult blessing.

Impulses he was never aware of he was now aware of, and he didn't know how to handle them.

It was easier to sit at a distance from a woman who could at any moment turn into a fox than it was to sit at a distance from himself who, for no reason at all, could at any moment turn murderous.

It damaged him to think that he was happier leaving the house in the morning than he was returning to it in the evening.

Once his door was an ordinary door, now it was a door with a fox pelt hanging from it. Once it shut out the world, now it opened into the world. It opened into himself.

One year, coming towards the shortest day, the mating season of foxes, he complained of a rank smell of fox in the house.

Saying nothing, she carried on.

Three nights later he said that he couldn't stand it.

On the night after that, his vexation intense, he sat as far off from her as he could.

Saying nothing, she went to the door, she took down the fox pelt. Going out, she draped it over her shoulders and, turning into a fox, she trotted away into the wild world. And so it was that from then on, the only human footprints the hunter ever saw were his own.

It happens, doesn't it?

A day comes when the world pushes open the door we have closed against it.

A day comes when we have to relearn ourselves and the world.

A day comes when, having written it on paper made from wood pulp, we must now rewrite our General Theory of Relativity on the fox pelt, this signifying out incipient allegiance to the suspicion that the universe is queerer than we can suppose.

Think of $E=mc^2$ draping the fox pelt it is written on over its shoulders – whatever it then becomes, that too is even more counter-intuitively true of the universe.

⋆⋆⋆   ⋆⋆⋆   ⋆⋆⋆

A shepherd he was, and always on May morning he would drive his sheep to higher grazing ground. No different this year than any previous year, he didn't need a dog to urge them on. As though they were glad to be free of the vexations of winter enclosure, they were lambs again, scampering and bounding upwards along old trails, up to new grass, up to what for them was their high home range.

Having nothing else to do, the shepherd sat on a turf covered rock, knitting a winter scarf for himself. Soon he saw a hare and then another hare. Finding each other, they stood on their hind legs and sniffed each other. The better to see them, the shepherd learned so steeply aside that his ball of thread rolled off his lap, down the hillside. Gone down to retrieve it, he saw to his utter surprise that it had disappeared through a great opening in the hill. For fifty years he had come to this hill, spending all summer long up here, he know it as well as he knew his own yard, and yet he had never caught sight of this opening. Had it just happened? Or was it that, normally closed to us, reality was now, for its own good reasons, opening up to us? If it was, he wouldn't be found wanting. He walked through and found himself in a great cavern. As though illumined by a light from within himself, he saw a royal, crowned figure lying asleep on an oak bed. How he didn't know, but he knew it was King Arthur. Arthur it was. Bright as his legend. Bright as our memory of him.

Beside the oak bed there was an oak table. On it there was a horn and a sword. Picking it up, he crashed the sword down on the table, making a sound much louder than he expected.

King Arthur awoke, lifted his head off the pillow, turned toward him and said, had you picked up the trumpet and blown it I The Once and Future King would have shaken off sleep, would have risen up and returned among people, the marvellous world as it used to be returning with me. Now I return to sleep. For centuries maybe. For longer maybe. Till someone finds the opening.

Disappointed and alarmed, the shepherd backed away, picking up his ball of thread as he did so. Back in the customary world he looked round, but, as though it had never been, there was now no opening in reality.

And so we ask, what has happened to Arthur in us? What has happened to what is right royal in us? What has happened to what is regal in us? What has happened to what is sovereign in us?

Peter: Did you see an old woman going down the path?
Patrick: I did not, but I saw a young girl, and she had the walk of a queen.

When and how did we lose that walk? How and when will we regain it?

I think of three horn calls: the horn call that will awaken Arthur and his world in us, the horn call that will awaken Morgan La Faye and her world in us, the horn call that will awaken Merlin and his world in us.

Arthur we can be.

Morgan La Faye we can be.

And Merlin, sage of the woods who sometimes comes among us speaking the twelve languages of the wind and the eighteen languages of the rain, him we can be.

Whoever you are, that's who you are, a young woman with the walk of a queen.

***   ***   ***

I went out to the hazel wood,
Because a fire was in my head,
And cut and peeled a hazel wand,
And hooked a berry to a thread;
And when white moths were on the wing
And moth-like stars were flickering out,
I dropped the berry in the stream
And caught a little silver trout.

When I had laid it on the floor
I went to blow the fire aflame,
But something rustled on the floor,
And someone called me by my name:
It had become a glimmering girl
With apple blossom in her hair
Who called me by my name and ran
And faded through the brightening air.

Though I am old with wandering
Through hollow lands and hilly lands.
I will find out where she has gone
And kiss her lips and take her hands;
And walk among long dappled grass,
And pluck till time and times are done
The silver apples of the moon,
The golden apples of the sun.

The question is: should we take this poem as seriously as we take $E=mc^2$? After all, we do live in a universe in which a caterpillar becomes a butterfly, allowing us to wonder whether what happens to a part of the universe cannot also happen to all of it. Could it be that even now our universe is in a cocoon it has spun for itself, is undergoing complete metamorphosis and will soon emerge as something unpredictably different?

It is like this. A man is getting ready to dissect the trout he caught that morning in the stream under his house. It is lying there dead, its eyes dead, on a marble slab. He turns to go to a grindstone to sharpen his knives but no sooner has he turned his back than he hears her, Trout Girl calling him by his name.

Or it is like this. I am lying anaesthetized on an operating table in the deep interior of a hospital. As though it was a double door, the surgeons have opened out my chest. While they are working on me she calls me. Calling out to them to stop, I get up off the table and, heart or no heart, I follow her, along corridors, across the yard, through the streets, out into her world, she as she enters every next wood or every next valley calling me to come out, to keep coming out of the deep anaesthetic of everyday hearing and seeing and knowing, and I do come out - out, out, out- and eventually there I am, back in my own yard, and I know looking at it that I will never get used to the wonder of it, of ass cart, of bucket, of thatch and calf, of my own door opening into my own floor, my chair by the fire a siege, a Siege Perilous, but bless me, bless my soul, I am worthy.

And if you ask me who that woman who lives with me is, if you ask me where she comes from, I will take down my fiddle from the wall, I will play one of Ireland's great airs for you, My Lagan Love, Roisín Dubh or Eibhlín a Rún, and as I play it I'll say to you, where this great air comes from, that's where she comes from, and it's where you come from, and it's where I come from. Where My Lagan Love comes from, that's where we all come from. Whether we know it or not, it is where all of us always abide.

And if you someday meet me coming out of an oakwood and you think I am Merlin, you will be right. Merlin I am, talking to you only about ordinary things, talking to you about wild duck or deer grass in one of the twelve languages of the wind or, it could be, in one of the eighteen languages of the rain.

Trout Girl: out of the anaesthetic of everyday hearing and seeing and knowing she calls us.

***   ***   ***

He was an inshore fisherman. He picked mussels and limpets and periwinkles from the rocks. He dug in the tidal sands for razor fish and cockles. As though led to them by a sixth sense, he harvested oysters and clams. And, rowing himself up and down the inlets, he fished with nets for shrimp when they were in season. Once, during an autumn spring-tide the wind was blowing from the land and when it did ebb the sea retreated farther than he had ever seen, out beyond three sea stacks, leaving only a shallow channel, loud with waders, in between. Greedily anticipating the rich pickings he would find, he crossed the channel, the birds taking affrighted flight, and he set to work. So absorbed did he become filling bag after bag, first with mussels and then with winkles, that he lost all sense of time and when, the last bag full, he looked up, he saw that the tide had turned and had cut him off. Having learned the hard way that he had no chance against currents so continuously swirling, he decided there was nothing for it but to sit it out until the next ebbtide.

Making his way to it, he sat in the lee of a great ledge of rock. Night came down. At the full coming up and then rising high in the sky, the moon was so bright it was almost like day. In the small hours he got up to work a stiffness and chill out of his body, out of his mind as well, and it was then he saw them, seals coming ashore, and the wonder of it was that, having struggled up onto the rock ledges, they dropped their seal coats and became human beings. Never had he seen their like for beauty, but what was yet more marvellous, they continually flourished in the wonder of each other. He watched them, entranced by them, till dawn. Till ebbtide. And then, like he was dreaming, like he was doing it in a dream, all thought of shellfish forgotten, he stole around, picked up one of the seal coats and started for home, walking hip deep across the channel.

Since, without her coat, the sealwoman couldn't turn back into a seal and swim away as all the others were now doing, she followed him, across the channel, up the shore, along the small roads, into his house. That night, after she had fallen asleep, he left their bed and went out and, leaning a ladder against it, he hid the seal coat in the thatch.

In time a child was born to them. And then another. And another.
Often, during those years, she would go down to the shore and while she was there, looking seaward, you might as well not talk to her at all or call her, for she wouldn't hear you.

One day, as she was kneading dough at a great board table, a drop of seal oil fell down into it. Getting the smell of it, it all came back to her, her life as a seal in the sea, her sons and her daughters in the sea, her grandmothers in the sea. Aching, knowingly now, to be with them, she crossed the yard to an outhouse, came back with a ladder, leaned it against the thatch, dug in it, and found her seal coat. Reaching the lip of the tide, she draped it over her shoulders, she became a seal, and was gone. Not forever though, for some mornings, looking at each other, her children on land will see that their hair has been combed in the night, her way of telling them that she has been back, and will come back.

With good reason, some of us settle for a little life. Never do we cross a channel at ebbtide. Never do we run the risk of being cut off from an acquired but fixed sense of who we are. Never, coming up out of our culture, do we drop our conditioning, all of it, leaving it behind us, unregarded, on the rocks. Sometimes it happens though. A drop of seal oil falls down into our fixed sense of ourselves and 'tis as if a spell has been broken.

Where we tend to see fixity the story sees fluency and the day will surely come when we will be happy to flow, not just from one to another identity but from identity as such, back into God.

***   ***   ***

Tegid Foel and Ceridwen were wed. A year later in a house that looked like a folktale had imagined it a daughter was born to them. Then a son. The son was as ugly as the daughter was fair. Hardly had they washed him and dried him than they called him Morfran, meaning Great Crow. Worse still. He grew every year more ugly and now, so as not to lie about him, they called him Afagdhu, meaning Utter Darkness. But Ceridwen, a nature goddess in disguise, so some thought – no, she was determined that her son would not be an outcast because of his ugliness. She would make him all-wise, and this, his wisdom, would ensure that he would be welcome at the tables of chieftains in their ringforts and of kings in their high, never to be conquered castles.

A cauldron Ceridwen had, and now, as at its making, she chanted a variety of spells, long and short, all of them in an unknown language, into it, all round inside it, all round outside it, into its rim. Herbs boiling water wouldn't boil these spells would boil, compelling them to yield up their most secret essences.

Intending to brew a drop of wisdom for Afagdhu, for him alone, Ceridwen charged Mordha, an elderly man, to procure the logs, and Gwion Back, a boy, him she charged to tend the fire, and this they must do every day for a year and a day. Also, every day for a year and a day, Ceridwen would herself go out into the world seeking the necessary herbs, some of them rare, some of them growing so briefly in places so occult that only someone with second sight would find them.

Things went well.

Sometimes in the night Ceridwen would dream of a herb and off she would go in the morning, her dream having shown her the way.

That's how it was, day after day, Mordha bringing in the logs, Gwion Back tending the ever fervent fire, Ceridwen coming home with the herbs, the cauldron boiling, not boiling itself away, not steaming away, everything kept within, a spell she had spoken having ensured this.

On the last night of the long wait Ceridwen dreamed of yet one more herb growing in an old heron's nest at the top of the tree in a wood far away. Determined to be home early, she set out early.

At the time she expected to be back but wasn't yet back there was thunder in the cauldron. Contained within the cauldron, it was thunder more thunderous than was ever heard among the open mountains. Then there was silence. Still terrified, neither Mordha nor Gwion Back reached in to collect the brewed drop of wisdom. Now again there was thunder, this time snarling, and angry, and as though it had been spat out, out over the rim of the cauldron came the drop of wisdom. It landed on Gwion Back's thumb. It burned him, he licked it and, instantly now, he was all wise, all knowing, all seeing, seeing endlessly into the past, endlessly into the present, endlessly into the future. What had been meant for Afagdhu, was his by accident. Imagining Ceridwen's wrath, he rushed out of doors, only just in time, for with a scream the cauldron burst, its boiling contents burning a path for itself down the hillside into the river below Gwyddno Faranhir's salmon weir. Downstream from there Gwyddno's horses came to drink and, too much for them, the power in the water killed them.

Soon Ceridwen was coming over the brow of the hill. Seeing the still steaming path down to the river, she guessed what had happened and now, as the bursting cauldron had screamed, she screamed. Gwion Back took to flight. Her wrath scorching herself and the grass under her feet, she set off in pursuit. Just as she was about to lay vengeful hands on him, he became a hare. Not to be outdone, she became a hound. Again, just as she was about to close her mouth on him he leaped and became a salmon in the river. Instantly, she was an otter chasing him down. Rising up, he became a bird of the air but there she was, a falcon bearing down on him. Overflying a farm yard with great heaps of winnowed wheat in it, he dropped down, a grain among millions. A match for him whatever he did, she plunged and, shedding her falcon form, there she was, a red-combed black hen eyeing the wheat grains, swallowing the one with a difference.

The bother was, back to herself in her house, she knew she was pregnant with him. She pregnant with defeat. With defeat for herself. With defeat for Afagdhu. And nine months to wait until she could lay hands on him. He taking from her, digesting her. He kicking her. No. No now. Not now. Now, for now, she wasn't a match for him. And one thing she knew: he would go to full term.

Three weeks overdue, she screamed him out into her waiting hands, but no, defeated by him still, she couldn't do it, she couldn't kill him.

Within hours, her strength returned to her, she stitched him into a leather satchel, she walked west to the sea and committed him, to her surprise with prayers, to an outgoing tide. Out, out, out he was carried. Out beyond view. Her anger more hurtful because more useless, she turned for home.

Days and years ran on. It was May morning and always on May morning there would be a first run of salmon in off the sea and up the river, tidal at first and then cascading.

Busy with more urgent tasks himself, Gwyddno asked Ellflin, his not so clever son, to go down to the weir and bag the netted salmon.

To Ellflin's dismay, there were no salmon and, turning for home, he could well imagine how angry his father would be when he gave him the news, and worse, known for his stupidity, he as he always was would be to blame. Dreading the encounter, he looked back in the hopeless hope that he might see a gleam of silver ascending the river. What he saw instead was a gleaming something hanging from the near weir pole. Intrigued, in a childlike way, he retraced his steps, the fully risen but still low sun picking out the marvel, whatever it might be. Afraid at first to touch it, it frightened him all the more when he figured that it was a satchel encrusted all over with barnacles and mussels and little flutterings of seaweed. Eventually, in the hope that he'd find something in it that would pacify his father, he lifted it off, down onto the deck, he unstitched it and, looking down into it, he saw a bright-browed wonder child, saw him and heard him, he singing poems, their words more real than the things they talked about, hawks and mountain avens, salmon and stars.

Now called Bright Brow, now called Taliesin, Gwion Back sings. Still in the satchel he sings:

> There is news of the macrocosm in us its microcosm.
> The richer we are in ourselves the richer our sense
> of the universe.
> What we come home to in ourselves we come home to
> in the universe.
> When we come home to soul in ourselves we come home to soul in
> the universe.

Walking away, and growing to full human height, he sings:

> Purpose in perceiving perverts perceiving.
> Self-will in perceiving perverts perceiving.
> A perceiver in perceiving perverts perceiving.

> Perceiving.

> Perceiving these mountains.

> Perceiving them beyond the wound of
> someone perceiving and something perceived.

> Perceiving is.

Perceiving these mountains in the unwounded

Oneness of God ...

It is a question that many adults in our culture might ask: what has happened to the wonder child in us?

And how come our culture didn't do for us what Ceridwen did for Gwion Back?

How come that it didn't stitch us into a second womb or cocoon and return us into the genius of the universe.

The universe in which a caterpillar becomes a butterfly.

The universe in which Gwion Back becomes a wonder child.

The universe which, for all we know, might already have spun a cocoon for itself.

It is what the story would teach us: better to trust the genius of the universe in us than to trust our trivial daily minds.

***   ***   ***

Moments there are.

There is the moment when we see something otherwise quite ordinary, such as smoke from our chimney, and we know, seeing it, that the universe is stranger, maybe queerer, than we can suppose.

The moment when reality opens or maybe it is our mind that opens, there being days when mind and reality are one and the same.

The moment when, hearing our name called, our census-form sense of ourselves falls from us.

The moment when a drop of seal oil falls down into our world and we know that our empirical experience of ourselves, whether as seal, woman or whatever, isn't the whole story.

The moment when we come upon the wonder child we might have been or, starting again, could yet be, becoming in time the great remembered bard of a people.

I think of it, the day when Orion stands at our door. Like a postman, he returns to us everything we have said about the universe.

Seeing how dumbfounded we are, he tells us that no, the universe doesn't recognise itself in what we say about it.

Observing our continuing perplexity he says, partial knowledge is nescience, and that is as true of our partial knowledge of ourselves as it is of our partial knowledge of the universe.

I think of it, the day when Prospero buried his book,
I think of it, the day when, just for the day,
     Francis Bacon buries his book called Novum Organum.
     Galileo Galilei buries his book called Siderius Nuncius.
     Isaac Newton buries his book called Principia Mathematica.
     Albert Einstein buries his book called The General Theory of Relativity.

Day when, night when, the universe shines thoroughly through the impairments of our thinking about it.
Day when, coming home, the Mental Traveller looks up and sees smoke rising from his chimney. After incarnations of seeking, sometimes hunting, he has found the place and the state of mind to set out from.

One day, yearning beyond Paradise, we will resist the call and the lure of the girl with apple blossom in her hair. And then, the trail he has given his name to descending beneath us, we will run the risk of honouring our purposed but wisely postponed rendezvous with Bright Angel.

EPHPHATHA

The Liturgy of Opening Our Eyes

In the Gospel according to St. Mark we see Jesus the healer at work:

> And again, departing from the coasts of Tyre and Sidon, he came unto
> the sea of Galilee, through the midst of the coasts of Decapolis. And they
> bring unto him one that was deaf, and had an impediment in his speech,
> and they beseech him to put his hand upon him. And he took him aside
> from the multitude, and put his fingers into his ears, and he spit, and he
> touched his tongue; and looking up to heaven, he signed, and saith unto
> him, Ephphatha, that is, Be opened. And straightway his ears were
> opened, and the string of his tongue was loosed, and he spake plain.

The Aramaic word stands out.
It is a word of three syllables, the stress falling on the first of them:

Eph'-pha-tha

The question to ask here is: how deaf to the wonder and terror and glory of
the world are those of us who can hear? How unable to express the wonder and
terror and glory of the world are those of us who can speak?
Think of how Thomas Traherne experienced the world as a child:

> The corn was orient and immortal wheat, which never should be reaped, nor
> was ever sown. I thought it had stood from everlasting to everlasting. The dust
> and stones of the street were as precious as gold: the gates were at first the end of
> the world. The green trees when I saw them first through one of the gates
> transported and ravished me, their sweetness and unusual beauty made my heart
> to leap, and almost mad with ecstasy, they were such strange and wonderful
> things. The men! Oh what venerable and reverend creatures did the aged seem!
> Immortal cherubins! And young men glittering and sparkling angels. And maids
> strange seraphic pieces of life and beauty! Boys and girls tumbling in the street,
> and playing, were moving jewels. I knew not that they were born or should die,
> but all things abided eternally as they were in their proper places. Eternity was
> manifest in the light of the day, and something infinite behind everything
> appeared, which talked with my expectation and moved my desire. The city

seemed to stand in Eden, or to be built in heaven …

Famously, Wordsworth describes our declension from this, our first Paradisal or celestial estate, into what he calls the light of common day:

> Our birth is but a sleep and a forgetting:
> The Soul that rises with us, our life's Star,
> Hath had elsewhere its setting,
> And cometh from afar:
> Not in entire forgetfulness,
> And not in utter nakedness,
> But trailing clouds of glory do we come
> From God, who is our home:
> Heaven lies about us in our infancy!
> Shades of the prison-house begin to close
> Upon the growing Boy,
> But He
> Beholds the light, and whence it flows,
> He sees it in his joy;
> The Youth, who farther from the east
> Must travel, still is Nature's Priest,
> And by the vision splendid
> Is on his way attended;
> At length the Man perceives it die away,
> And fade into the light of common day.

For all that, Edwin Muir reminds us that we can grow back, however briefly, into Paradisal perception:

> Those lumbering horses in the steady plough,
> On the bare field – I wonder why, just now,
> They seemed terrible, so wild and strange,
> Like magic power on the stony grange.
>
> Perhaps some childish hour has come again,
> When I watched fearful, through the blackening rain,
> Their hooves like pistons in an ancient mill
> Move up and down, yet seem as standing still.
>
> Their conquering hooves which trod the stubble down
> Were ritual that turned the field to brown,
> And their great hulks were seraphim of gold,

Or mute ecstatic monsters on the mould.

And oh the rapture, when, one furrow done,
They marched broad-breasted to the sinking sun!
The light flowed off their bossy sides in flakes;
The furrows rolled behind like struggling snakes.

But when at dusk with steaming nostrils home they came,
They seemed gigantic in the gloom,
And warm and glowing with mysterious fire,
That lit their smouldering bodies in the mire.

Their eyes as brilliant and as wide as night
Gleamed with a cruel apocalyptic light.
Their manes the leaping ire of the wind
Lifted with rage invisible and blind.

Ah, now it fades! It fades! And I must pine
Again for that dread country crystalline,
Where the blank field and the still-standing tree
Were bright and fearful presences to me.

William Blake, it seems didn't need to reacquire Paradisal perception. No, it would seem, the shades of the prison-house didn't close upon him:

> The atoms of Democritus
> And Newton's particles of light
> Are sands upon the Red Sea shore
> Where Israel's tents do shine so bright

He assured us that if the doors of perception were cleansed, everything would appear to us as it is, infinite.

As for Yeats, it wasn't so much that he experienced a cleansing or an opening of the doors of perception, rather was it that he blazed ontologically:

> My fiftieth year had come and gone,
> I sat, a solitary man,
> In a crowded London shop,
> An open book and empty cup
> On the marble table-top.

While on the shop and street I gazed
My body of a sudden blazed;
And twenty minutes more or less
It seemed, so great my happiness,
That I was blessed and could bless.

And there is that strange night not just of silver branch perception but of ontological epiphany described for us in Moby Dick:

Days, weeks passed, and under easy sail, the ivory Pequod had slowly swept across four several cruising-grounds; that off the Azores; off the Cape de Verdes; on the Plate (so called), being off the mouth of the Rio de la Plata; and the Carrol Ground, an unstaked, watery locality, southerly from St. Helena.
It was while gliding through these latter waters that one serene and moonlight night, when all the waves rolled by like scrolls of silver, and, by their soft, suffusing seethings, made what seemed a silvery silence, not a solitude; on such a silent night a silvery jet was seen far in advance of the white bubbles at the bow. Lit up by the moon, it looked celestial; seemed some plumed and glittering god uprising from the sea.

Tonight, on board a whale ship named for an exterminated tribe, we do not have to take Manannan Mac Lir's word for it. Tonight we see and know reality as the sea god sees it and knows it. His Gita is the sea's Gita is our Gita. As he sings atoms sing, their auroral sonance their reality.
In a sense, it is what Manannán said to Bran:

> Ephphatha
> Be opened

Be opened in instinct, eye and mind and you will see that the physics of the silver branch is the physics of atoms, is the physics of rocks, is the physics of flowers, is the physics of stars.
His own transfiguration is Christ's Gita, is Christ's Zohar, an ontology. Press him on the issue on that day and he will tell you that not only is the lily of the field clad in glory, it is glory. Ontologically, it is glory.

Isaiah speaks:

In the year that king Uzziah died, I saw also the Lord sitting upon a throne, high and lifted up, and his train filled the temple. Above it stood the seraphims; each one had six wings; with twain he covered his face, and with twain he covered his feet, and with twain he did fly. And one cried unto another, and said, Holy, holy, holy, is the Lord of hosts: the whole earth is full of his glory. And the posts of the door moved at the voice of him that cried, and the house was filled with smoke. Then said I, Woe is me! for I am undone; because I am a man of unclean lips, and I dwell in the midst of a people of unclean lips: for mine eyes have seen the King, the Lord of hosts. Then flew one of the seraphims unto me, having a live coal in his hand, which he had taken with the tongs from off the altar: and he laid it upon my mouth, and said, Lo, this hath touched thy lips: and thine iniquity is taken away, and thy sin purged. Also I heard the voice of the Lord, saying, Whom shall I send, and who will go for us? Then said I, Here am I, send me.

And what we wonder was his iniquity, what his sin?

What our iniquity, what our sin?

In the event that we are iniquitous, it must sure have its source in our inability or in our unwillingness to see that the earth doesn't only reflect God's glory, it is full of it, it is fun-filled, filled-full of it.

Where there is no vision, expect moral failure.

Contrarywise, where there is silver branch perception and a sense of silver branch being, it is likely that there will be silver branch morality.

It sometimes happens that many people together emerge simultaneously into silver branch perception, into a silver branch sense of being. It happened to the knights of the Round Table four hundred and fifty four years after the passion and death and resurrection of Christ:

> And than the kynge and all the astatis wente home unto Camelot, and so wente unto evynsong to the grete monester. And so aftir upon that to sowper, and every knight sette in hys owne place as they were toforehonde.
>
> Than anone they harde crakynge and cryynge of thundir, that hem thought the palyse sholde all to-dryve. So in the myddys of the blast enfyrde a sonnebeame, more clerer by seven tymys than ever they saw day, and all were alighted of the grace of the Holy Goste. Than began every knight to beholde other, and eyther saw other, by their semynge, fayrer than ever they were before. Natforthan there was no knight that might speke one worde a grete whyle, and so they loked every man on other as they had bene doome.
>
> Than entird into the halle the Holy Grayle covered with whyght

samyte, but there was none that might se hit nother whom that bare hit. And there was all the halle fulfilled with good odours, and every knight had such metis and drynkes as he beste loved in thys worlde.

And whan the Holy Grayle had bene borne thorow the hall, than the holy vessel departed suddenly, that they wyst nat where hit becam. Than had they all breth to speke, and than the kyng yelded thankynges to God of Hys good grace that He had sente them.

Pentecost Sunday though it was, the Grail today and for now was covered in white samite and so, seeking a more open vision of it, these knights on the morrow rode through the street of Camelot and soon they had entered the dark wood of the world, a wood of paths more perplexed and perplexing than any of them, ever, even in dreams, had to take on. Here be witcheries. Here be sorceries suave and savage. Here be enchantments.

Here, treacherously, nothing is what it seems. Here, showing himself to be the fairest of maidens, is the great red dragon whose scream, when he does scream, quenches all fires in all realms near and far. Here be Nightmare and her Ninefold. Here, lying across your path, and looking ordinary, is a piece of deadwood that Nightmare herself, for fear of losing her already mad mind, wouldn't step over. Here, in this dark wood, it wouldn't be wise to rely on a pentangle of virtues blazoned on banner, shield and coat, or, as they would be spelled in adventurous times past, on banere, shelde and cote. The knyghtes of the Table Rounde have entered the heart of darkness. On a later adventure, it was with good reason that Sir Gawain prayed,

Cros Kryst me spede

Along some of its reaches the spiritual quest is an anious vyage.
Virtues we heraldically paraded at tourneys and parleys we won't parade now. Alone and without such prestige in the dark wood we find out what we are made of.

Walpurgis Nacht is the shadow side of Whitsunday.

Whytsonday at Camelot. First there was a crakynge and a cryynge of thundir.

And how greatly would we mistake this were we to think of it as meteorological thunder. This is the Grail Realm announcing itself. Next, seven times clearer than the light of day, the light and grace of the Holy Ghost enters the hall and settles on the seated knights, transfiguring them and rendering them speechless. Finally, filling the hall with heavenly fragrances, the Holy Grail enters. Mercifully, it is preciously covered, for who otherwise could endure the radiance. A blessed vessel, it moves around the Round Table and, under the species of whatever meat and drink each knight best likes, it distributes heavenly sustenance.

Objectively, that is what happened in Camelot on Whitsunday. Subjectively, we can think of it as the coming of Paradisal perception, because the Grail isn't only a thing, it is a way of perceiving no matter what thing, a shoe or a star. And that means that the knights didn't have to ride out in quest of it. It is as available right there in Camelot as it is elsewhere. It is as available to Yeats in a tea shop in London as it is to Edwin Muir, rustically roofed, in the Orkneys. Everything the knights saw Jacob Boehme saw, in a pewter dish.

Ephphatha\
Be opened

Be opened and behold\
Think of the apocalyptic 'Behold':

Behold, a great wonder in heaven, a woman clothed in the sun, with the moon under her feet, and on her head a crown of twelve stars.

Healed of the anaesthetic built into our senses, all beholding, all perceiving and knowing, is apocalyptic. Wherever we happen to be, we look at an old boot, and we know that's it,

Paradisal perception is ours

The Grail Quest is accomplished.

Without a corresponding morality it will all have been in vain.

MANTRA PRACTICE

Think of the apocalyptic 'Behold':

Behold, a great wonder in heaven, a woman clothed in the sun, with the moon under her feet, and on her head a crown of twelve stars.

Heavenly wonder though she is, there will be those who will not continue to merely behold her. In passionate devotion to her, they will yearn to grow in likeness to her. Not even content with this, as her bhaktas they will yearn to merge with her, anticipating all of which, and seeking to realize it, they will chant an enabling mantra

> Maria'ham
> Maria'ham
> Maria'ham

Over and over and over again they will chant it

> Maria'ham
> Maria'ham
> Maria'ham

Bhaktas of Jesus will chant an equally enabling mantra:

In baptismal assimilation to Jesus the Christ I live
In baptismal assimilation to Jesus the Christ I live
In baptismal assimilation to Jesus the Christ I live

Over and over and over again they will chant it:

In baptismal assimilation to Jesus the Christ I live
In baptismal assimilation to Jesus the Christ I live
In baptismal assimilation to Jesus the Christ I live

Let us have liturgically con-forming mantras. Mantras that con-form us to the great occasions of the liturgical year.

For instance:

It is Christmas morning in my nature now

It is Easter morning in my nature now

Today, as the Apostles were, I am Pentecosted

Jesus was born on what Yeats calls the bestial floor. To say therefore that it is Christmas morning in my nature now is to say that it is Christmas morning in all that I am, in instinct as well as in intellect and, in spite of so much else that might go so terribly wrong, what a happy Christmas that is!

It is Christmas morning in my nature now
It is Christmas morning in my nature now
It is Christmas morning in my nature now

Sing it in February, in August, in October, whenever or wherever you feel like it.

I think of Christians who, because of their confidence in Christ's redemptive work, resort more readily to mantra than to petitionary prayer:

Lotus I am, opened out to the love of God I am
Lotus I am, opened out to the love of God I am
Lotus I am, opened out to the love of God I am

In another mood, in another situation, someone might say:

Surrender to God I am
Trust in God I am
Psalm 24 I am

The Lord is my shepherd, I shall not want...

AGONY IN THE GARDEN

In a dream of it, the Garden of Olives was a Garden of Myths. Of myths that enact us in our phylogenetic precipitousness. And Jesus was Endendros, the one who suffers in the tree. It wasn't because it was autumn that these myths, dendromorphic and fruiting, were so hectic.

Hectic the dendromorphic Minotaur myth:

It was as if, overnight, the world had regressed to the way things were in the beginning. What would formerly happen to us only in sleep was happening to us now awake.

One morning, in Crete of the Mountain Mother, in Crete of the ships prowed with Out Lady of the Snakes, a bull came up out of the benedicting sea. In him, rippling tyrannically at sirloin and lowing larynx, was the instinctive life we had suppressed in the interest of civility. Instantly, at sight of him, the heifer nearest to him in the Royal Meadows was in heat. Going to her, he smelled her under her slightly arched tail, he licked her there and, raising his head, and drinking it with his slime-wet nostrils, he drew the smell of her back and down into him, back as far as his loins and down into his hooves. This he did a second time. This he did a third time. Then, shadowing her hips with his head, he mounted her and, after three big thrusts, he slid back off her.

Downwind from him one day, Pasiphae, the queen, picked up the smell of him and, whatever the consequences, in heaven or on earth, she too must be mounted.

She visited Daedalus, cleverest of men.

Next evening, after sunset, Daedalus invited her to back into the hollow likeness of a cow.

Its timbered, all-fours shape, suited her perfectly.

It only remained for him to cover it in cow-hide and to smear its rear-end with vulva slime from a cow in heat.

It worked.

The bull came. He smelled her, licked her, mounted her and, she lowing, he showered her inwardly to her swelling nipples and to her hoofed finger-tips.

Nine months later she gave difficult birth to a bull-chested, bull-headed child. Civility being what it then was, she didn't have the nerve to keep and rear her baby in the palace.

And so it was that Daedalus impounded him in a Labyrinth under our politeness in the literal sense of our good-mannered way in a polis or city. Suppressed, the baby grew in and into anger, his bull-mind crowding his man-mind, his man-mind driving his bull-mind, both minds muscled together. In a dream of him that she had, he looked at his unsucked mother with eyes as red, and as hungry for that kind of thing as butcher shops. Strange, the butcher shops traded only in veal, and that was a portent, because, as well as growing in anger and brutality, the monster grew in delicacy. A delicate taste in food he had. A taste for veal. The veal not of calves. An earthquake that must be fed he was. And he held the whole world to ransom, threatening it unless the black-sailed shiploads came. And they came, they came, they came, until in the end, no veal available, we settled for the big one, the big bellowing, the quake.

Hectic the dendromorphic Andromeda myth:

Long ago, in a land far away and but little known to the rest of the world, Kepheus was king and Kassiopeia was queen.

One day, not altogether unaware of the enormity of the sacrilege she was committing, Kassiopeia boasted that she was more beautiful than the Nereids, those divine maidens, lovely and enchanting, who live in the sea. In revenge, Poseidon, thunderous and earthquaking when he needed to be, he, Lord God of the sea, sent an inundation as long as its longest river against the land.

Watching it withdraw, Kepheus knew that, unless he did something to redress the wrong, more and worse would follow.

Consulting an earth-oracle he learned that, by way of expiation, he must expose Andromeda, his daughter, to the instinctive good pleasure of Ketos, the Sea-Beast.

In sad but determined compliance, he chained her, her thighs
spread wide for easy violation, to a rock low down on a savage
shore.

The Beast had already engulfed her in his five squid-suckering arms when, swooping down on Pegasus his winged horse, Perseus speared him through his wide-open, watering, vermilion mouth.

Hectic the dendromorphic Hippolytus myth:

Sired by Theseus his father on a one breasted warrior woman, Hippolytus was heir to the throne in Troezen, a sea-side city in Greece of the Centaurs and horse-yarded Satyrs. At a time when other young men knew they were men and wanted to be men, Hippolytus would go off alone to gather flowers and make coronals for Artemis, the fiercely because precariously chaste goddess of wild animals, wild places, and the hunt.

Hipploytus too, he was fiercely because precariously chaste, and so it was that he never once contrived to be alone in the palace or in the fields with a girl of his own age.

To hunt where Artemis hunted, to hunt in wild places, that was his joy, his exceeding delight.

Aphrodite, goddess of the tumescent embrace, her he disdained.

Slighted, it pleased Aphrodite to encompass his destruction.

Foreseeing consequences, she saw to it that Phaedra, his step-mother, would burn, would flame and burn, with incestuous love for him.

Being who she was, daughter of Pasiphae and half-sister to the impounded Minotaur, Phaedra flamed and, consequences not a consideration, she would have the virgin boy, if not in the palace, then in the wilds where he hunted.

Her advances savagely and repeatedly rejected, she ailed, she pined.

With much persistent and clever questioning her nurse divined the cause of Phaedra's fall from good health and, in innocent hope of remedy, she went to Hippolytus.

In a rage that reddened to outrage, Hippolytus threw door after palace door open, threw open the doors of the royal bedchamber and confronted her. Seeing how beyond all hope her passion was, and vengefully seeking to redeem her honour, Phaedra cried out, help! help! help! I am ravished! Cried it until she lay on the floor and actually believed that she was being ravished!

Ravished!

Ravished!

by the virgin boy she burned for.

Recovered, she hanged herself, leaving a letter of accusation for Theseus, her husband.

That night Hippolytus was banished and seeing him go in his four-horse chariot, Theseus his father asked Poseidon his grandfather to destroy him.

As Hippolytus, the young prince, blameless in his own eyes, was riding north along the coast road, Agrian Teras, a Beast white and vast, erupted from the sea and panicked the horses into blind uncontrollable flight. Crushed, again and again, against the wayside rocks, the chariot was broken to pieces and, entangled in the reins, Hippolytus, favourite of Artemis, doomed by Aphrodite, was dragged to long-drawn-out red hippolution.

Hectic the dendromorphic Actaeon Myth:

Actaeon was a hunter. To an extent that frightened even them, he was often of one mind with his hounds.

One day, of one mind and mouth with them, he sprung a lone stag. Antlers he saw. A shimmer leaping a stream he saw. Eruptions of dust and skirmishes of dust he saw. And this was it. This was what he had reared and fed his hounds for. This was what he had broken in his horse for. This was what he himself was born for. It was what he lived for. And now, out here in the country turned up by boars, never by the plough, he knew. By the foam-softened howling he knew that it wouldn't be long till the stag stood at bay. Suddenly, and unaccountably, there was silence, and, as though horrified, his mare reared. And reared and reared, refusing utterly to be mastered. And to add to his sense of the pure stupidity that will sometimes show up in things, there they were, his hounds coming back, in twos and threes coming back, all lust for the hunt, all lust for the kill, gone out of them.

There being nothing else he could do that day, Actaeon tightened his right reins and turned for home.

But that wouldn't be the end of it. That couldn't be the end of it. That stag, the noblest he had ever seen, must stand at bay. At bay to his hounds. At bay to his pride in himself.   At bay to his pride in his mare

That stag at bay!

At bay!

Sitting high, bringing only his three roughest hounds, he set out.

All morning, it was a canter through country he knew.

The stag, he was sure, hadn't come back within the home horizon, so he kept going, ignoring every temptation to give chase to lesser quarry. By the time his shadow was at its shortest and he was merged with it almost, it was country not known to him that he was riding in. Country Saggitarius, when he was among us, might have hunted in. Country Orion, when he was among

72

us, might have hunted in.

Suddenly, as though a chasm had opened before him, his horse reared. Reared and reared, and neighing, screeching more than neighing, she wouldn't be mastered. And, mastered by something unknown, his hounds wouldn't budge. Determined that this time he would have his way, Actaeon dismounted and, to show horse and hounds that there was no border he wouldn't cross, he strode forward in a calm, red rage.

On and on he strode. On and on until, stopped short by the brink of a river, he looked down and unable now not to see her, he saw Artemis and her nymph's swimming in a pool. Outraged in this her nakedness to mortal eyes, Artemis, the divine and virgin huntress, turned the full fury of her gaze upon him, turning him, the hunter, into a stag. Downwind from him, his hounds picked up the scent and, released from holy hesitation, they howled, howled, howled. In mortal danger, and knowing it, Actaeon broke for open ground. But these were his roughest hounds. They had been bred to give chase and not to give up. It was in his own yard, his door closed against him, that they brought him down. Driving them off before they got to it, a servant severed the big, antlered head and on the fourth day following it looked down, wide-eyed, but not seeing Artemis, from the ancestral chimney breast. And that's it, the story of a hunter of animals engulfed by the animal in himself. And how terrible when, poisoned by repression or by over-insistent civility, the collectively engulfing animal is

Beast

Hectic the dendromorphic Oedipus Myth:

Laius was king in Thebes. Unable to get to the bottom of a portentous dream, he consulted the earth-oracle at Delphi and was told that a son, due soon to be born to Jocasta his wife, would murder him. Six nights after he was born, Laius stole his son, spiked his feet and exposed him in the wolfish hills. A shepherd who found him took him to the king of Corinth who happily received him into his household.

Here, his wet nurse named him Oedipus, meaning Fraught Foot.

Grown to be a man, he set off into the world.

On a high road one day, he refused to yield ground to a man in a cart. They fought and, to day, for the first time, Oedipus found that there was murder in him.

He threw the corpse, not all its wounds fist wounds, to the gathering eagles and hawks.

On an age-old royal road down into Thebes, he was challenged by the Sphinx.

A faintly smiling hybrid, the Sphinx had the head and breasts of a woman, all else was crouching lion, the tail tapping, indolently tapping, the ground in front of her.

Showing up on all the roads in and out of it, the sphinx had sentenced Thebes to a slow death, indeed she had sentenced civilization to a slow death, because, unless you solved the riddle she put to you, she killed you.

Her tail indolently tapping, she challenged Oedipus:

> What is it that walks on four legs when young, on two
> legs in middle life and on three legs in old age?

Clever man that he was, Oedipus didn't fall for the trick in the riddle, that trick being the utter obviousness of its solution. Instead of backing away from the obvious and looking for something more recondite as everyone else had done, he, having the nerve for the obvious, simply announced the obvious: man, he said, is the answer to your riddle because, in infancy we get about on all fours, in middle life we walk on two legs, and in old age on three legs, the third being a walking stick.

Defeated, the Sphinx leapt to her death over the precipice garlanded with the corpses of all the men and women who had come this way, to them recondite. Entering Thebes by its seventh gate, Oedipus was hailed as a saviour, as the hero who, able for the obvious, had reopened the road to civilization and culture.

By popular demand, he married the widowed queen and was crowned king. Children were born to them and, watching them grow, no one could doubt that theirs was a dynasty like none other.

A chastisement from the gods, everyone said of it, said of the plague that so suddenly and with so many sickles struck the city, struck it and prospered in it, finding suppurating lodgings in every house.

Seeking the cause, Oedipus took things in hand.

His eyes used to looking away from himself and therefore in the wrong direction, he got nowhere.

One day, recovering his nerve for it, he saw and announced the obvious:

> I, Oedipus, am son to Laius the man I murdered on the high road. I am husband to Jocasta my mother and that means that I, the saviour, the hero, who re-opened the road to civilization and culture, am incestuous half-brother to my sons and my daughters.

74

In brief:

I, your saviour, am your plague.

Oedipus walked out of civilization into his own myth, and so implicitly thereafter did he credit it that where he should have felt the extrusive burgeoning of fins he deludedly felt the intrusive disturbance of spikes.

Final anagnorisis eluded Oedipus Tyrannus.

For Jesus it was a night of utter wakefulness to our humanity in all its possibilities. As Nietzsche who recoiled from it will attest, it is no small matter to suffer and survive such wakefulness. It is no small matter to inhabit us wholly and holily in all that we Jurassically and Messianically are, especially when we remember that the Messianic impulse will all too readily give rise to kinds of frightfulness unknown in the Mesozoic. As wise as he needed to be during that more than nocturnal night, Jesus wasn't the dupe of his own goodness.

Believing that it will help us to cross the Torrent with Jesus, we listen to the Mandukya Upanishad in Christian translation.

THE MANDUKYA UPANISHAD

A CHRISTIAN TRANSLATION

Why else except in the hope of sanctity would I continue to live, I one day asked myself, and with that I walked out and walked up along our river, all the way up to its headwaters and it's here, in a herd's house, that I have lived ever since.

The perversity of it, I thought. To be born for conversation and to have no one to converse with. To be the kind of man that a woman would fall for and here I was, higher than cowslips and grouse, going to bed alone.

Some mornings the mountains were numerously murderous. Put a foot wrong up there on one of those ridges and all the way down along a jagged fall you'd be hung up in morsels convenient for carrion crows. And worse altogether it would be, up here, to put a foot wrong inside of your mind.

Other mornings, trusting to what your eyes saw not to what your mind knew, you'd be tempted to set out and walk through these same mountains, thinking them to be accumulations and shapes of pure blue soul.

On such mornings to impute meaning to the world was to impugn the world. I called all meanings home, and that was the most dangerous and the most reckless thing I had so far done in my life.

It was a shock to discover how infested with meanings my eyes and mind had been.

Not eclipsed by meaning, the January moon brightened my yard with a light not sheathed in adverb or adjective.

Shining, but not through our astronomies, the stars would some nights look like they had it in for the Earth. Even in my water-butt, water that mirrored them had a wounded taste.

It was tough going, fasting not from this or that minor instinct, fasting from a chief instinct, our instinct to meaning.

Having no mirror, I could only imagine how emaciated my eyes and mind looked.

Going to bed at night, knowing that it was ahead of me anyway, I would willingly surrender to dreamless sleep, meaning that I was willing to forfeit all sense of my own existence, meaning that I was willing to give up being me, to give up being anything at all, to give up being.

Meditating three times a day, I would seek to be as ascetic awake as I was in dreamless sleep. Achingly, I had an anaesthetic sense that in such anaesthetic self-abeyance I was next door to God. More. I was available to take-over by God.

Awake, the self-abeyance was never complete. Self couldn't dissolve self. The best I could do was to turn the work over to God. My part was to be annihilatingly available.

It was how I understood the horror of Jesus on Golgotha.

It was in baptismal assimilation to him that I continued.

When it came, inwardly and outwardly the catastrophe was ragnarok big. In an instant, long as forever, I underwent utter dis-illusion-ment, compelling me to inherit a Hindu estimation of mind and world. It was like waking up in and within dreamless sleep: mind as source of the world-illusion and the world-illusion itself, both were gone, and I was a terrorized trembling in the nothingness.

It was ruination of a kind that I couldn't have anticipated. And even if they were Siberian shamans or Viennese psychoanalysts, there was no point in calling the king's horses, no point in calling the king's men.

Soon there was something else I came to know. There is in the human body a physical appendix into which its poisons drain. Similarly, there is in the human psyche a karmic appendix and in me now it had burst, flooding my mind, fogging my eyes, my room, my windows. What was so ruinously frightful was that the horror-images were impulse-images.

They were impulsions to action.

Naively, I gave myself a year to come through. Seventeen years later, out of the blue, it would be as though I had drunk the wine of astonishment, as though I had yet again drained the dregs of the cup of trembling.

Sometimes I would ask myself, must nearness to God mean ruination? Is that what Golgotha means?

I would think of Jesus, his head collapsed onto his chest, his meaningless eyes looking down into his own empty skull.

Fantastically, I would dare to believe that Golgotha isn't exaggeration. The Passion from beginning to end isn't exaggeration.

Christ in Gethsemane, Christ on Golgotha, Christ in the Garden of the Sepulchre, how surprised I was that all of this made sense to me. How surprised I was at how soon it became visual vocabulary to me.

Just my luck to find myself baptismally reassimilated to Christ in his Passion, that at a time when, chiefly perhaps because of its scenic horror, people were walking out of it.

Stellar astronomy.
Starless astronomy.

The starless astronomy of Good Friday.

The blessed catastrophe of the empty skull.

It is worth it.

Days there are.

   Up here, higher than primroses and grouse, but not always higher than hell,
it is what I mean by making the sign of the cross on myself.

    Shantih   Shantih   Shantih

Faith, we believe, has its reasons

As Your Faith Is So Will You Become

The Maitri Upanishad has it that

> As is thy thought, so dost thou become;
> This is an everlasting mystery.

The Bhagavad Gita has it that

> Faith is connatural to the soul
> Of every man:
> Man is instinct with faith:
> As is his faith, so too must he be.

The Dhammapada has it that

> What we are today comes from our thoughts of yesterday, and our
> present thoughts build our life of tomorrow: our life is the creation of
> our mind.

In the Timaeus, Socrates has this to say

> Now, when a man abandons himself to his desires and ambitions,
> indulging them incontinently, all his thoughts of necessity become
> mortal, and as a consequence he must become entirely mortal, because
> he has nourished his mortal part. When on the contrary he has earnestly
> cultivated his love of knowledge and true wisdom, when he has primarily
> exercised his faculty to think immortal and divine things, he will – since
> in that matter he is touching the truth – become immortal of necessity,
> as far as it is possible for human nature to participate in immortality.

The Elder Brother, a character in Milton's Comus, speaks as it were from a
Puritan pulpit:

> So dear to heaven is saintly chastity
> That when a soul is found sincerely so
> A thousand liveried angels lackey her,
> Driving far off each thing of sin and guilt,
> And in clear dream and solemn vision

Tell her of things that no gross ear can hear,
Till oft converse with heavenly habitants
Begin to cast a beam on the corporeal shape,
The unpolluted temple of the mind,
And turns it by degrees to the soul's essence,
Till all be made immortal. But when lust,
By unchaste looks, loose gestures and foul talk,
But most by lewd and lavish act of sin,
Lets in defilement to the inward parts,
The soul grows clotted by contagion,
Imbodies and imbrutes, till she quite lose
The divine property of her first being.
Such are those thick and gloomy shadows damp
Oft seen in charnel vaults and sepulchres
Lingering, and sitting by a new-made grave,
As loth to leave the body that it loved,
And linked itself by carnal sensuality
To a degenerate and degraded state.

Fervently, if not hectically, Blake says

If the Spectator could Enter into those Images in his Imagination, approaching them on the Fiery Chariot of his Contemplative Thought, if he could Enter into Noah's Rainbow or into his bosom, or could make a Friend and Companion of one of these Images of wonder, which always intreats him to leave mortal things (as he must know), then would he arise from his Grave, then would he meet the Lord in the Air and then would he be happy.

Calmly, as if it had worked for himself, Yeats says

There is for every man some one scene, some one adventure, some one picture, that is the image of his secret life, for wisdom first speaks in images and … this one image, if he would but brood over it his whole life long, would lead his soul, disentangled from unmeaning circumstance and the ebb and flow of the world, into that far household, where the undying gods await all whose souls have become simple as flame, whose bodies have become quiet as an agate lamp.

Six mahavakyas or great sayings which suggest that human nature isn't the unalterable fatality that we sometimes experience it to be.

Relevant here is something Pico della Mirandola has to say in his Oration on the Dignity of Man:

O supreme generosity of God the Father, O highest and most marvellous felicity of man! To him is granted to have whatever he chooses, to be whatever he wills. Beasts as soon as they are born (so says Lucilius) bring with them from their mother's womb all they will ever possess. Spiritual beings, either from the beginning or soon thereafter, become what they are to be for ever and ever. On man when he came into life the Father conferred the seeds of all kinds and the germs of every way of life. Whatever seeds each man cultivates will grow to maturity and bear in him their own fruit. If they be vegetative, he will be like a plant. If sensitive, he will become brutish. If rational, he will grow into a heavenly being. If intellectual, he will be an angel and the son of God. And if, happy in the lot of no created thing, he withdraws into the centre of his own unity, his spirit, made one with God, in the solitary darkness of God, who is set above all things, shall surpass them all.

Also, observing that custom can and often does become second nature, Pascal wondered whether nature itself is only a first custom.

If nature is indeed only a first custom, a first habit or nexus of habits, then presumably we can challenge it as we would any secondary habit or addiction and, improbable as it might seem, maybe we can break it. Astonishingly, on the morning of his enlightenment, the Buddha sings not of his restitution or resurrection but of his own utter self-executed demolition in body, in mind and in his sense of being a self:

Through many lifetimes, incarnate
And discarnate, have I toiled,
Seeking but not finding
The builder of the house.

Housebuilder, I behold you now;
Again a house you will not build.
All your rafters are broken now,
The ridgepole also is destroyed.
My mind, its elements dissolved,
The end of craving has attained.

From which we insecurely conclude that the self which builds up an identity over many lives has now destroyed not only that identity but itself also. And this apparently is what liberation means. The ruined and dissolved identity and the dissolution of the need or the craving to be an identity – that is what he, who no longer is an identity, is celebrating.

It has been said of course with good reason that it is as difficult for a self to destroy itself as it is for a fingertip to touch itself.

Far otherwise is it with mystics who understand themselves to be involved in a gracious journey back into God.

We only have to think of Al Hallaj who, nearing the end of his journey, prayed to God whom he believed to be gracious:

Between me and Thee there is an 'I am' that torments me. Ah! Through Thy 'I am' take away my 'I am' from between us both.

As though Marguerite Porete had prayed such a prayer and it had been answered, she says of our final condition that it is like being in God without being oneself.

But, for those of us who aren't ecstatic to ourselves in God it might be a good idea to go back to where we started.

As you sow, Jesus says, so shall you reap. Socrates goes further, insisting that as we habitually think and do so shall we become.

That custom, that conduct, can become second nature or even primary nature in me is a truly alarming idea. Ultimately it means that since in my thinking and doing I demiurged it, nature in me neither is nor will be my alibi. Since I am responsible for nature in me I am also responsible for what it drives me to do. Edmund in King Lear is wonderfully brutal on this point, he saying

'tis the excellent evasion of whoremaster man to lay his goatish disposition to the charge of a star.

So, not only am I responsible for who and what I will become, I am responsible also for who and what I have become, all the way back perhaps through countless existences, not all of them incarnations.

Nietzsche would challenge Edmund, saying:

I have discovered for myself that the old human and animal life, indeed the entire prehistory and past of all sentient being, works on, loves on, hates on, thinks on in me.

Am I responsible for what Aurignacian warriors think in me? Am I responsible for what Australopithecus Africanus thinks in me? Am I responsible for what tyrannosaurus rex thinks in me? Am I responsible for what trilobite and ammonite think in me, dream in me? Am I responsible for what the first amino acids think in me, dream in me?

Answering his own questions, Nietzsche might say: much that I am I lay to the charge of Magdalenian, Jurassic and Precambrian life in me.

Going further, he might say: not only am I not responsible for the total phylogenetic totem pole I in some sense am, by night in my dreams, by day in my dealings with the world, I am its victim.

It is why Christianity is right in putting Passion where it does, in the depths, at the forefront of things.

Jesus says of himself, before Abraham was I am, but in Gethsemane he will discover what Oedipus even in anagnorisis didn't discover, the primogeniture of the fin in his feet and hands and the primogeniture of the reptile brain in his bright brow.

To suffer the awful actuality of such primogeniture is, in the Christian sense, Passion.

It is the passion of 'is' and 'ought', of Jurassic savannah 'is' and summit of Mount Sinai 'ought'.

To Plato and Pico I say, any intellectual seeds I sow are subsequent and superficial to vegetative and sensitive seeds already sown, genetically sown.

The difference between Passion Narrative and Upanishad is that, aware of the extent to which we are thought and dreamed and driven by our reptile brain, the Passion Narrative cannot so confidently say, as is thy thought, so dost thou become.

A Christian who says, it is Easter Morning in my nature now, is likely also to be saying, it has, over years, been Holy Thursday at night in it, and, yet more dreadfully, it has, in what seemed like eternity, been Good Friday at noon in it.

Unlike the Maitri Upanishad a Christian Passion Narrative will have reservations, one of them the fin in our feet and hands, another of them our reptile brain.

Speaking to him out of a whirlwind, his God put it to Job that the hope of Leviathan is in vain. This suggests that the hope of old Ordovician and Jurassaic life in us is in vain.

In spite of so much evidence to the contrary, a Christian dares to believe otherwise.

A Christian dares to believe that it wasn't in vain that Jesus crossed the Torrent.

As a Christian sees it, it makes more than metamorphic or regenerative sense to cross the Torrent with Jesus. It makes final evolutionary sense to do so.

AUGURY OF INNOCENCE

It was when I looked up and saw the Unicorn walking towards me that I realised I had crossed out of a brutal way of seeing and being in the world.

He was pure.

In his purity there was extreme intolerance and, for me, extreme danger.

And yet I was glad. Sight of him suggested that I had served my time in the Labyrinth and in the Canyon and now I had graduated from a world expressed and oppressed by the Minotaur into a world expressed by the Unicorn.

As though he assumed that I wasn't yet ready, he avoided me widely, came back to the path, and kept going.

I sat in the lee of what was clearly a metamorphic erratic in limestone land and I thought things through.

To emerge from the Canyon is not to climb up out of it and say goodbye to it forever.

It is within the Canyon that we emerge from the Canyon.

To begin with, suspending my disbelief, I trespass into Blake's way of seeing things:

The atoms of Democritus
And Newton's particles of light
Are sands upon the Red Sea shore
Where Israel's tents do shine so bright.

Going further, I practice the belief that the subatomic particles of which I am physically made are hosannas, are self-sounding quavers in the everlasting song of the heavenly hosts. Joining them, I sing with them:

Holy, holy, holy, Lord God of hosts,
    Heaven and earth are full of your glory

Apocalyptically heard by Isaiah when he walked into the Temple of Solomon in Jerusalem in the year that King Uzziah died, this song is called the Kedushah in Hebrew, the Trishagion in Greek and the Sanctus in Latin:

Sanctus, sanctus, sanctus, Dominus Deus Sabaoth,
pleni sunt caeli et terra gloria tua.

In the subatomic, self-sounding quavers of brainstem, spleen and sperm I am

Kedushah, Trishagion, Sanctus.

Sanctus, sanctus, sanctus, Dominus Deus Sabaoth,
pleni sunt caeli et terra gloria tua.

In brain tumour, femur and phlegm I am Kedushah, Trishagion, Sanctus.

Sanctus, sanctus, sanctus, Dominus Deus Sabaoth,
pleni sunt caeli et terra gloria tua.

And the Maitri Upanishad assures us that as our faith is so are we. And the Bhagavad Gita agrees, saying that as our faith is so must we, so will we, become. And the teeth, all canines, of tyrannosaurus, what of them? What of them at the moment when they close upon the chest of a smaller reptile – physically smaller but bigger than the universe in fright? Is that mouth at that moment a Gloria of Gregorian quavers? Is that mouth at that moment sanctus? Below what either is aware of, are crushing mouth and crushed chest a Kedushah in two-part harmony? Presiding Genius at the Marriage of Heaven and Hell, Blake by implication says yes, says everything that lives is holy.

The trouble with this is that Blake's is a shallow heaven and a shallow hell, and it is said that love is blind but marriage is an eye-opener:

It is not easy to fall out of the hands of the living God:
They are so large, and they cradle so much of a man.
It is a long time before man can get himself away.
Even through the greatest blasphemies, the hands of the living God still
continue to cradle him.

And still through knowledge and will, he can break away,
man can break away, and fall from the hands of God
into himself alone, down the godless plunge of the abyss,
a god-lost creature turning upon himself
in the long, long fall, revolving upon himself
in the endless writhe of the last, the last self-knowledge
which he can never reach till he touch the bottom of the Abyss
which he can never touch, for the abyss is bottomless.
And there is nothing else, throughout time and eternity
but the abyss, which is bottomless,
and the fall to extinction, which can never come,
for the abyss is bottomless,

and the turning plunge of writhing of self-knowledge, self-analysis
which goes further and further, and yet never finds an end
for there is no end,
it is the abyss of the immortality
of those that have fallen from God.

Not that D.H. Lawrence thought of this as an epithalamion written in direct
response to Blake's prothalamion.   But how instructive it is to read them in
sequence. There's a hell that Blake's heaven and hell have no inklings of.

So what now?   Now that we have opened the door of our logos about
anthropus to Beast and Abyss? To Demon, Beast and Abyss?

Going down into it, Jesus redemptively endured the abyss of the immortality
of those that have fallen from God. Mentally, as Tibetan Buddhists would, do we
set up a shrine to him in each and every one of our darkest impulses, praying to
him to commence and complete the work of their sanctification? Reposing total
trust in him, do we go down to the floor of the Karmic Canyon and, sitting lotus-
like there, do we practice being in Paradise?

Are not Blake's four lines an open gate back into Paradise? Is it not by opening
our eyes that we cross back into Paradise?

The atoms of Democritus
And Newton's particles of light
Are sands upon the Red Sea shore
Where Israel's tents do shine so bright.

Esoteric to Blake's lines is a famous passage from the Book of Deuteronomy:

A Syrian ready to perish was my father, and he went down into Egypt, and
sojourned there with a few, and became there a nation, great, mighty and
populous: And the Egyptians evil entreated us, and afflicted us, and laid upon
us hard bondage: And when we cried unto the Lord God of our Fathers, the
Lord heard our voice, and looked on our affliction, and our labour, and our
oppression. And the Lord brought us forth out of Egypt with a mighty hand,
and with an outstretched arm, and with great terribleness, and with signs, and
with wonders: And he hath brought us into this place, and hath given us this
land, even a land that floweth with milk and honey.

To sing or recite Blake's visionary lines in the Canyon, to sing them in the
hearing of Democritus and Newton, is to challenge them and ourselves to emerge
not from hard bondage under Pharaoh in Egypt but from hard bondage under

Medousa here at home. Medousa doesn't only have teeth in her mouth. Always needing to analyse things, to break things down into their constituents, she has teeth in her eyes, teeth in her mind. Unable ever to simply see things, she chews things into sight of things, into knowledge of things. In this she is Muse of modern science.

The question is: how can Medousa shed her shining dentition of eye and mind? How can Medousa become who she Paradisally was? How can Medousa become Miranda?

Without teeth are Miranda's eyes and mind.

I imagine a language that sees things as Miranda sees them. In it the root meaning of every word, even the word Medousa, is Miranda.

Who will be our Muse, Medousa or Miranda?

It is something like a Fall we are talking about, our fall from Miranda to Medousa to Minotaur.

Medousa and the Minotaur: chewing perception and brute passion. In initial mythic estimation they are what we are up against in ourselves. To practice being Miranda, to practice being in Paradise, comes neither naturally nor easily to us. And yet, there are days when without having willed it, we have returned from chewing perception to still seeing. There are days when, corresponding to how we ourselves are, Nature is revelation not veil. Not even that. There being no veil, there is no unveiling, no re-veil-ation. Nothing in us quavers. Sanctus is seeing, not singing. And now, not fearful for us, the Unicorn turns and walks three steps of our way with us.

To day again.

Anything I might add to pure seeing, to Torc Mountain as it appears in pure seeing, would be impoverishment. Add a Mozart andante and it would be impoverishment.

To day I understand the Fall. Not content with innocence prior to experience, Adam and Eve set out in quest of innocence in and through experience.

To day I pity Paradise.

Going up to its growling gate I call in, come out into the greater wonder.

What I mean is this: given the pits of hell we so recurrently dig for ourselves, given the yet deeper hell we go down into, it is no longer sufficient to aspire only to Paradise Regained. Dreadfully, more than dreadfully, we must aspire to a Paradise without walls. Dreadfully, more than dreadfully, we must aspire to where we are.

A CHRISTIAN ORPHEUS

We know him as St. Ciarán of Saighir, one of Ireland's earliest Christians. It is said that he met St. Patrick in Rome. Sensing a kind of saintly outlandishness in him, Patrick gave him a hand-bell, telling him to go home and set up a monastery wherever it rang unrung. It rang, unrung, in a wilderness scarce in everything except savagery.

Reverent remembrance, already old in the eight century, loves his story:

The blessed Ciarán took up his habitation like a hermit in the waste, for all about was a waste and tangled woodland. He began to build his little cell of mean stuff, and that was the beginning of his monastery. Afterwards a settlement grew up by God's gift and the grace of the holy Ciarán. And all these have the one name, Seir.

Now when he came there he sat down under a tree in the shade of which was a boar of savage aspect. The boar seeing a man for the first time fled in terror, but afterwards, being tamed by God, it returned like a servant to the man of God. And that boar was Ciarán's first disciple and served him like a monk in that place. For the boar immediately fell to before the eyes of the man of God and with his teeth stoutly severed branches and grasses to serve for the building of the cell. For there was none with the holy man of god in that place. For he had fled to the waste from his own disciples. Then came other animals from the lairs of the waste to the holy Ciarán, a fox, a badger, a wolf and a stag. And they abode with him as tame as could be. For they followed the commands of the holy man in all things like monks.

One day the fox, being more subtle and full of guile than the rest, stole the slippers of the abbot, the holy Ciarán, and turning false to his vow carried them off to his old earth in the waste, designing to devour them there. And when the holy Ciarán knew of this, he sent another monk or disciple, the badger, to follow the fox into the waste and to bring his brother back to his obedience. So the badger, who knew the ways of the woods, immediately obeyed the command of his elder and went straight to the earth of brother fox. He found him intent on eating his lord's slippers, so he bit off his ears and his brush and tore out his hairs. And then he constrained him to accompany him to his monastery that there he might do penance for his theft. So the fox, yielding to force, came back with the badger to his own cell to the holy Ciarán, bringing the slippers still uneaten. And the holy man said to the fox: 'Wherefore, brother, hast thou done this evil thing, unworthy of a monk?

Behold! Our water is sweet and common to all. And if thou hadst a desire of thy natural craving to eat flesh, the omnipotent God would have made thee flesh of the bark of trees at our prayer.' Then the fox, craving forgiveness, did penance fasting, and ate nothing until the holy man commanded. Then he abode with the rest in familiar converse.

Afterwards his own disciples and many others from every side gathered about the holy Ciarán in that place; and there a famous monastery was begun. But the tame creatures aforesaid abode there all his life, for the holy elder had pleasure to see them.

What a charming end to our battle with the Beast in ourselves and in the world! Ciarán and badger and boar and fox and stag and wolf singing matins together in a little thatched church in the wilderness, its door antler high and wide to nature inside and outside us:

Caeli enarrant gloriam Dei, et opera manuum ejus annuntiat firmamentum

Singing lauds together:

Cantate Domino canticum novum, cantate Domino omnis terra.
Cantate Domino, et benedicite nomini ejus: annunciate de die in diem salutare ejus.
Annunciate inter gentes gloriam ejus, in omnibus populis mirabilia ejus...

Singing nones together:

Jubilate Deo omnis terra: servite Domino in laetitia.
Introite in conspectu ejus, in exultatione.

Singing vespers together:

In illa die stillabunt montes dulcedinem et colles fluent lac et mel, alleluia, Euouae.

It must be that Ciarán was at ease with animal nature in himself, else the boar-brutal, fox-vicious, stag-shy animals of the wilderness wouldn't have been so happy to sing Nunc Dimittis, bringing Compline to an end, with him:

Nunc dimittis servum tuum, Domine, secundum verbum tuum in pace, quia viderunt oculi mei salutare tuum, quod parasti ante faciem omnium populorum, lumen ad revelationem gentium et gloriam plebis tuae, Israel.

Bethlehem and Saighir or, as it is phonetically rendered in the text, Seir.
Over the centuries, Christians have become used to Bethlehem, to the idea of two domesticated animals, an ox and an ass, breathing warmth on a wonder-child lying in their manger.

But what of Seir? What of two savage animals, a wolf and a boar, what of them singing matins? What of them, before they go back to their monastic cells at night, singing Simeon's Song of Salvation:

Now, O Lord, lettest thou thy servant depart in peace, according to thy word, for mine eyes have seen thy salvation, which thou hast prepared before the face of all people, a light to lighten the Gentiles and the glory of thy people, Israel.

A wolf! With predatory eyes! Breaking off from the hunt and seeing salvation – with those eyes?

Is this the Messianic outcome of history and of creation as the Bible foresees it?

Is it that, here in Seir, Ciarán and the animals are already living that outcome?

The wolf shall dwell with the lamb …

The lion shall eat straw like an ox

The sucking child shall play on the hole of the asp and the weaned child shall put his hand in the cockatrice's den.

There will be no hurt on God's holy mountain.

A sense I have is that there is something quite different going on in Seir.
The sense I have of him is that Ciarán is a Christian Orpheus.
In his nature, in all of it, not just in part of it, he has emerged into the Orphic note and that is why the animals, savage like the boar and shy like the stag, are happy to sing it with him.
Not that it is all Orphic plain sailing in Seir.
When it does eventually happen, the regression, while comic, is serious, especially so in the case of the badger.
One day there it was, another bowl of vegetable soup set before the fox. Looking down into it, his mouth wearied and watered for flesh, for bleeding, hot

raw flesh deep as his teeth. In his mind he had a hare in sight, his nostrils drinking her smell. Mightily he resisted the impulse and soon again he was calm, the soup, as it so often did, tasting like penance. Next day, passing his cell door, he saw that the abbot had left his slippers outside to dry in the sun. Thinking that he might find the taste of hide in the leather, he yielded to his instincts and made off with them and before he knew what was what he was back to his old ways in his old earth in the wood.

No sooner had badger entered the earth than he too regressed, turning snarlingly savage, biting off the fox's ears, biting off his tail, tearing the fur from shoulder and belly. Never, during all those years in the wild, had he fought as ferociously as he did now, in the interest, seemingly, of monastic law and order.

So what then of the Orphic note? Does it exist? And if it does, are there people who in their very being become it? Is it immanent in all of nature, in rocks, in animals, in stars? Is the universe but a blossoming of it? Is it an astronomical exuberance of it? Is it the eternal divine silence in its adventure into sound that we are talking about? Is that what the Orphic note is, the sound of the eternal divine silence, that sound solid in rocks, stellar in stars? And when someone reverts from sound to silence, will wolf and badger and boar and fox and stag, as by impulsion from an awakened instinct that lessens established instincts, will they turn of their trails, following what is now their chief desire, to be sym-phonic with it?

To be symphonic with it in Ciarán of Seir is to be symphonic with it in themselves. In Seir, to be symphonic with it as sound is to be symphonic with it as silence. The boar and the stag who were symphonic with it as sound at matins, at lauds, at nones, at vespers an at compline, were symphonic and maybe homeophonic with it as the eternal divine silence.

It should be remembered as a great day – the day a handbell rang unrung in Ireland.

And Seir? Seir is the bindu, the centre of the Mandala, the place of universal emergence and return.

And Ciarán? As Ogma once was, Ciarán is now the philosophical question. To understand him is ultimate understanding of all things.

In Ireland, St. Ciarán's Christianity preceded the Christianity of St. Patrick. Isn't it time we gave it precedence in other than a temporal sense? In this of course, even in thinking about it, we must remember that it was Patrick who gave the hand-bell to Ciarán, and so, in fairness, the question of precedence must remain undecided. What is important is that, having been a founding bell, the hand-bell could be the bell of refounding.

Christianity isn't only a morality that has its source in divine command.

As well as so much else that it presumably was, at Seir Christianity was the lived apprehension of unity in plurality out of which an ecumenical morality prospered. Ecumenical not just among human beings of different persuasions and languages. Ecumenical across all boundaries, among all species living and extinct, among all worlds visible and invisible.

And as for what happened to Brother Fox and Brother Badger, well, yes, it happens to individuals, it happens to tribes, it happens to civilizations and we only have to look at the one we live in to know that it happens to worlds.

As Christ born on the bestial floor does, as Christ in the Canyon does, Ciarán of Saighir suits our world.

In Slí na Fírinne we run the risk not just of Christian ontology but of Christian anthropology.

DEINANTHROPUS

A New First Stasimon

Fifteen years ago or so, when I was still living in Connemara in the west of Ireland, I heard that there was a dinosaur exhibition in the zoo in Dublin. It occurred to me that Lorna and Sara my godchildren, who lived in the big house across the yard from me, might like to go and see it. I put the idea to them and instantly they were delighted and could hardly wait, and so it was that two days later Lynne, their mother, waved good bye to us in Galway train station. Three hours later a friend of ours met us on our arrival in Dublin, took us first to her home for lunch and then to the Zoo. No sooner had we entered the Mesozoic than Lorna and Sara took off, two little tots from the far evolutionary future crossing Triassic savannahs, making their way through Cretaceous forests, coming back to find me and lead me in excited safari to where he was, and yes, there he was, Tyrannosaurus Rex, terrible in his teeth, in his roaring terrible, and tall enough they told me to look in at them at night through the window of their first floor bedroom back in Connemara.

That room I knew well. In it all rabbits were bunny rabbits, all bears were teddy bears. In it all tigers and lions were cuddly and, what is more, every nursery rhyme that Sara and Lorna knew tiger and lion and rabbit and bear knew:

> There was a crooked man
> Who walked a crooked mile;
> He found a crooked sixpence
> Upon a crooked stile.
> He bought a crooked cat
> Who caught a crooked mouse,
> And they all lived together
> In a little crooked house.

But now, his mouth a Mesozoic slaughterhouse, Tyrannosaurus Rex had looked through their little Miss Moffet window and I wondered whether with that their Song of Innocence hadn't become a Song of Experience.

Next day, coming home in the train, they turned the table between us into a Jurassic savannah, at the heart of it all the Tyrant himself, he the might-is-right Rex in red roaring.

What I thought but didn't say to the girls is that now, a hundred million years later, kingship in killing has passed to us. On a whale-ship we see, in any of our slaughterhouses on land we see, in Verdun, in Auschwitz, Hiroshima and Dresden we see, that compared to us ichthyosaur, pterosaur and dinosaur are small fry. Sitting at home that night I listened to two roars, the Mesozoic roar of Tyrannosaurus Rex and the Kainozoic roar of the Colosseum.

Of the two roars the more recent is surely the most frightful. But why ? Is it that it has something extra in it ? Something hellish ? Nero's thumb turned down has in it something not found in the eye-tooth of a tiger.

I thought of Boehme's anthropology. I thought in the literal sense of his logos about anthropus:

In man is all whatsoever the sun shines upon or
heaven contains, also hell and all the deeps.

Only beings who have hell in them can make life a hell-upon-earth for others.

Only beings who have heaven, earth, hell and all the deeps in them can deepen hell.

And the big achievement of European humanity in the twentieth century is simply that: we deepened hell. Auschwitz is a tenth circle of hell that Virgil and Dante didn't go down into and that for the reason that it didn't yet exist.

The abyss that opened in Lucifer is shallow compared to the abyss that has opened in us.

On the assumption that we are what we claim to be, sapient, it behoves us to take stock.

It behoves us to hear and heed

The Psalmist who says
I am fearfully and wonderfully made.

Heraclitus who says
You would not find out the boundaries of the soul, even by
travelling along every path, so deep a measure does it have.

Jacob Boehme who says
In man is all whatsoever the sun shines upon or
heaven contains, also hell and all the deeps.

Sir Thomas Browne who says
There is all Africa and her prodigies in us

William Law who says
Thy natural senses cannot possess God or unite thee to Him;

nay, thy inward faculties of understanding, will and memory
can only reach after God, but cannot be the place of His
habitation in thee. But there is a root or depth in thee from
whence all these faculties come forth as lines from a centre,
or as branches from the body of the tree. This depth is called the
centre, the fund or bottom of the soul. This depth is the
unity, the eternity – I had almost said the infinity – of the soul;
for it is so infinite that nothing can satisfy it or give it any rest
but the infinity of God.
William Blake who says
In your bosom you bear your heaven and earth and all you behold.

Wordsworth who says
                                Not chaos, not
        The darkest pit of lowest Erebus,
        Nor aught of blinder vacancy scooped out
        By help of dreams – can breed such fear and awe
        As fall upon us often when we look
        Into our Minds, into the mind of Man –

Baudelaire who says
        Homme libre, toujours tu cheriras la mer.
        La mer est ton mirroir; tu contemples ton ame
        Dans le deroulement infini de sa lame,
        Et ton esprit n'est pas un gouffre moins amer.

Nietzsche who says
        I have discovered for myself that the old human and
        animal life, indeed the entire prehistory and past of all
        sentient being, works on, loves on, hates on, thinks on in me.

Emerson who says
        It is the largest part of man that is not inventoried.
        He has many enumerable parts: he is social, professional,
        political, sectarian, literary, in this or that set or corporation.
        But after the most exhausting census has been made, there
        remains as much more which no tongue can tell. And this
        remainder is that which interests.

Hopkins who says

O the mind, mind has mountains, cliffs of fall
Frightful, sheer, no-man-fathomed. Hold them cheap
May who ne'er hung there----

William James who says
    The further limits of our being plunge, it seems to me,
    into an altogether other dimension of existence from
    the sensible and merely understandable.

D.H.Lawrence who says
    There is that other universe, of the heart of man,
    that we know nothing of, that we dare not explore.
    A strange grey distance separates
    our pale mind still from the pulsing continent of the
    heart of man.

    Forerunners have barely landed on the shore
    and no man knows, no woman knows
    the mystery of the interior
    when darker still than Congo or Amazon
    flow the heart's rivers of fullness, desire and distress.

Joseph Conrad who says
    The mind of man is capable of anything – because
    everything is in it, all the past as well as all the future.

Rilke who says
    However vast the outer space may be, yet with all its sidereal distances, it
    hardly bears comparison with the dimension, with the depth dimension of
    our inner being, which does not even need the spaciousness of the universe to
    be within itself almost unfathomable.

Cumulatively, these mahavakyas, these great sayings, enact a Copernican revolution in anthropology. In them and with them we migrate from a Ptolemaic to a Boehmean sense of human inwardness, from a sense of human inwardness as bounded and therefore containable and controllable by ego and will to a sense of it as more or less boundless and therefore un-containable and uncontrollable by ego and will.

Think of what Nietzsche discovered: that homo habilis thinks in him, loves in him, hates in him; that australopithecus africanus thinks in him, loves in him, hates in him; that pterosaur, ichthyosaur, dinosaur, crinoid, crab, trilobite, ammonite, alga – that all of life all the way back through the Kainozoic, Mesozoic and Palaeozoic thinks in him, loves in him, hates in him; that the first protein thinks in him, loves in him, hates in him; that his consciousness is Jurassic, Silurian, Precambrian; that it is Cretaceous as well as classical; that it is dryopithecine as well as Dionysian; that it is Permian as well as Apollonian.

And yet, in all of this he has merely discovered but a little of who and what he is, he has merely discovered who and what he phylogenetically is. Beyond all of this, Jacob Boehme came to know what isn't biological in us: heaven in us, hell in us, deeps in us.

When palaeontologists began to seriously classify fossils they invariably denominated them by combining appropriate Greek words. So it was that they combined deinos and saurus, thus getting dinosaur, meaning terrible lizard.

The reality of who and what we are demanding it, it would be wise on our part were we to put deinos and anthropus together, thus getting the noun deinanthropus and the adjective deinanthropic, words suggesting immensities of biological and parabiological inwardness.

To migrate from an anthropic to a deinanthropic sense of ourselves – that from our first emergence has been the next evolutionary move or mutation that has awaited us.

Western history makes one thing profusely and prodigally evident: it is perfect folly to go on devising a culture for ourselves, to go on legislating for ourselves, on the obviously false assumption that we are anthropus, the truth being that we are deinanthropus.

In cultures not suited to us it is inevitable that what is deinanthropic in us will continue to blow up in our anthropic faces.

It's a dilemma.

For the reason we have suggested, it is perilous to live anthropically, to live in and from the more or less secure sense that inwardness is, by and large, the domain of ego, troublesome at times, but mostly manageable. It is on the other hand equally if not more perilous to live deinanthropically, to live, as so many mystics have, in full exposure to inner immensities, immensities into which and over which the ego's jurisdictive writ does not run.

What to do ?

By way of an answer, initial and inadequate, I will rehearse a dream that dreamed me as I slept one night in what by day was a room with a view down along a suave salmon river.

I am walking down Charring Cross Road in London. I turn into Old Compton Street. A little way along, drawing gaudy attention to itself on the far side, is a striptease club that I used to frequent, years ago, when I first lived in this city. Crossing the street, I go in. I am immediately as it were becalmed. No effort involved, I emerge into a state of silent wonder. The wonder is altogether older and deeper than I am. The individual I am, or was, is dissolved in the silent sea of it. And yet a ghostly suggestion of who I am survives in it. Independently of who I am the wonder is wondering at the great and marvellous transformation that has taken place here. Gone is the old chiaroscuro. Gone too are the lurid allurings to priapic delight. Vaguely, I am aware of striptease music upstairs, but it is the Salome veils in my eyes and mind that are falling away. They do fall away, all seven of them, and now I see what I have been looking at. On this sunlit, paradisally bright ground-floor where I am are rack after rack after rack of summer clothes all of them also paradisally bright, suggesting paradisal innocence regained. All living instincts in me are becalmed in the wonder of them. And wonder beyond words it is when I see that they are all unisexual. For a long while, forever it seems, I am timeless, charmed beholding. With no sense of loss, I turn away and come back out into the street. Walking towards Wardour Street, I am aware that I have a four-pronged farm fork in my hand. On the prongs are scales of dry dung, cow dung or dinosaur dung I cannot say. Turning into it,

I walk up Wardour Street. Naturally like one state of mind succeeding another, I am in an eighteenth century city park. Here everything is reasonable, the grass perfect, the trees and shrubberies as ordered as rhyming couplets. Now again, naturally, as I am walking in it, farm fork in hand, this perfect park becomes Eocene savannah. I do not see them, but I think there are hominids in the bushes. They are watching me. Maybe Lucy is watching me. A long way into the savannah I notice a patch of ground that is older than its surroundings. Now I know why I have the farm fork, the manure fork, a digging fork it turns out to be. I begin to dig. One after the other I uncover three steeply descending granite steps. Each step seeming to be a geological era, the first kainozoic, the second Mesozoic, the third Palaeozoic, I climb down and, alarmed by what might happen next, I stand on what paradoxically is a precipitous height, on a sheer geological rock-wall height, in the depths. Below me, endlessly far down in geological time, is an old sea, mere more than sea. From where I stand everything I see is afar. So far away, down and away, is the far embankment that I could never ever reach it by travelling towards it. As from nowhere, there is a man standing at the edge of it. Bending forward from the hips, he sinks his hands down into the sea, if sea it is. The merest gesture, the merest mime, of lifting on his part is all that is needed. Up it comes, a great sea-wide iron grid, breaking the surface of the water. Up and up it comes, the far side rising, folding itself in flush with the rock-wall I am standing on. Invisibly deep in the archaic sea something tremendous is happening. Strangely, before I see it, I know what it is. Up from the depths, a tremendous, ageless, boiling, green and blue, breaking to turquoise, is rising. Even before it breaks the surface, I see that it is an immense confusion or tangle of sea zoas, zoas of the benthos. Draped across them all, undulating downwards out of view and upwards into view, in a kind of continuous infinite, is the Great Zoa himself, a stupendous, endless snake form. Seeing him, I call him a dogfish. Such a pleroma of surgent, insurgent life in any one being I have never seen. Thunders and taigas bloom under the snake-patterned, gorgeous geographies of his skin. Under it, undulating as he does, are summer tundras and tropical rainforests. All things outrageous and insolent in time and eternity are teeming there. Somehow I take my entranced eyes off him. I am standing on the far embankment, where the man who lifted the grid stood. I am barefoot. An otter comes towards me. Afraid that he will bite my small toe I back away. I am sitting on the water, exactly where the confusion of sea zoas rose. Behind me, eyeing me, his vast canyon-coloured mouth agape, and watering for me, is a lizard-like living enormity. Not needing to look around to see him, I see that he is getting voraciously ready to lunge at me and swallow me. His mindless mind made up, he backs back so as to have a better run at me. Fully agape, his mouth a canyon, he charges forward to engulf me but, at the very last moment, as though playing with me, he veers away to the right of me. Backing furiously, he shakes auroras off himself. Showing off he is. He steadies himself. Now again, the canyon his mouth is, I see it, watering for me. He comes at me but, still playing with me, he veers away, this time, at the last moment, to the left of me. That's it, I think, the rehearsals are over. Back at the starting point he positions himself. Gaping as only a canyon at nightfall can, he comes at me. Resigned, I wait. This time, as I expect, there is no veering to left or right. I am engulfed, but somehow I am not swallowed. I open my eyes. I am sitting there, in daylight. Not needing to look, I see that the canyon-mouthed enormity has become a harmless little creature, harmless and shy, going off about his business in a nearby reed bed. I wake up.

A journey along Old Compton Street into what Joseph Conrad might call the heart of human darkness.

A journey up an inner Amazon or Congo into what D.H.Lawrence has called 'that other universe, of the heart of man'.

In a way that Lawrence for the moment doesn't seem to be, Conrad is calmly not hectically alert to the possibility of a frightful outcome. Ascend Old Compton Street or ascend the river, be it the Thames or the Congo, and you are running the risk of ending up as Kurtz did, a demon of the place, enthroned and worshipped.

The verdict on the Christian Light Bringer, the Christian Lucifer, is

The horror !   The horror !

And yet the dream suggests that the repressing grid can go up and, however great the threat to us, we are in the end not engulfed, not even harmed. It suggests that we can go down into our oldest psychic sea and not only can we settle there, we can flourish from there.

The good news from the psyche itself is this: we don't have to always live superficially, from above the repressing grid. Without risk of harm to ourselves or to others, we can live from the oldest phylogenetic roots of who we are.

It is the humanism of no matter what human being walking along Old Compton street with a karmic digging fork in his or in her hand.

But Conrad is right. We can, like Kurtz, dig our way down into fantastic trouble. On the way down, what happened to Nebuchadnezzar can happen to us. We can regress to the animal, or worse, to the beast, in us:

> The same hour was the thing fulfilled upon Nebuchadnezzar: and
> he was driven from men, and did eat grass as oxen, and his body
> was wet with the dew of heaven, till his hairs were grown like eagles'
> feathers, and his nails like birds' claws.

We can lift up the repressing grid but only to see the suddenly insurgent id usurp the ego as in prophetic vision it will usurp Idumea:

> But the cormorant and the bittern shall possess it: the owl also and the raven shall dwell in it------and thorns shall come up in her palaces, nettles and brambles in the fortresses thereof: and it shall be an habitation for dragons and a court for owls. The wild beasts of the desert shall also meet with the wild beasts of the island, and the satyr shall cry to his fellow; the screech owl also shall rest there, and find for herself a place of rest. There shall the great owl make her nest, and lay, and hatch, and gather under her shadow: there the vultures also shall be gathered, every one with her mate.

A reversal of Freud's hope, that being that where the id is the ego shall be.

As for Conrad, he alerts us to the possibility not just of beastly but of demonic usurpation:

The thing was to know what he belonged to, how many powers of darkness claimed him for their own. That was the reflection that made you creepy all over. It was impossible – it was not good for one either – trying to imagine. He had taken a high seat among the devils of the land – I mean literally. You cant understand. How could you ? with solid pavement under your feet, surrounded by kind neighbours ready to cheer you or fall on you, stepping delicately between the butcher and the policeman, in holy terror of scandal and gallows and lunatic asylums – how can you imagine what particular region of the first ages a man's untrammelled feet may take him into by the way of solitude – utter solitude without a policeman – by the way of silence – utter silence, where no warning voice of a kind neighbour can be heard whispering of public opinion ? These little things make all the great difference. When they are gone you must fall back on your own innate strength, upon your own capacity for faithfulness. Of course you may be too much of a fool to go wrong – too dull even to know you are being assaulted by the powers of darkness. I take it, no fool ever made a bargain for his soul with the devil: the fool is too much of a fool, or the devil too much of a devil – I don't know which. Or you may be such a thunderingly exalted creature as to be altogether deaf and blind to anything but heavenly sights and sounds. Then the earth for you is only a standing place – and whether to be like this is your loss or your gain I wont pretend to say. But most of us are neither one nor the other. The earth for us is a place to live in, where we must put up with sights and sounds, with smells, too, by Jove – breathe dead hippo so to speak, and not be contaminated.

Over centuries in medieval Europe there was astonished talk about a single spear cast that destroyed a realm. I sometimes think that Conrad's parable is such a spear cast. Not that it has destroyed a realm but how can it not have pierced our confidence in our ability to see to it that there will never again be an Auschwitz. I think of a new Luther who would nail the parable not to a door in Wittenberg but to a door in Brussels, the one behind which Europeans are now devising a constitution for themselves.

Coming as he does from Brussels, Kurtz should be portent.
It has been said of Shelley, the English revolutionary poet, that he was an ineffective angel. It has been said of his work that it lacks greatness because he, its author, lacked a vision of evil. Yet he did say:

O thou who, plumed with strong desire,

Wouldst float above the earth, beware!
A shadow tracks thy flight of fire,
night is coming.

Thinking of our European flight of fire to a brave new world of our own devising – not only has that flight of fire been shadowed, the shadow has many times overtaken it, has many times engulfed it, pulling it down into Verdun, into the mud of Flanders, into Sophie`s choice, into Dresden.

What is this shadow?
Not lacking a vision of evil, it is likely that Conrad would initially say what we have already heard him say:

The mind of man is capable of anything – because everything is in it, all the past as well as all the future.

In other words, as Nietzsche discovered, the human mind is Silurian, it is Jurassic, it is Eocene. Or, to say it yet more graphically, the raised up sea-beds of the Grand Canyon in Arizona are the still living, still active, sea–beds of the human psyche.

Notoriously, a German Biologist named Haechel advanced the now discredited theory that ontogeny recapitulates phylogeny, meaning that in the womb each one of us undergoes the entire course of evolution all over again. To put it crudely, we evolve from being a tiny protozoan, to being fish, to being amphibian, to being reptile, to being mammal, to being simian, to being human.

A theory discredited by scientists might however have ad hoc value in our efforts to understand ourselves. Certain it is that some of us are born with gills and some with tails. Certain it is that the smell brain of the first mammal is alive and well in us. Also, we only have to part our lips to see our simian dentition, our simian eye-teeth. On the ad hoc assumption that we have indeed emerged through all these evolutionary stages, is it not conceivable that we will sometimes regress to one or another of them, this making us comprehensible to ourselves when we behave like sharks, crocodiles, when we show our teeth as baboons do.

There are Greek myths that know what we aren't always consciously willing to know.

Think of Pasiphae regressed to bovine all- fours.

Think of the Minotour her bull-chested, bull-headed, bull-natured son. In him all that we phylogenetically are has outcropped more or less all over all that we ontogenetically are.

Think of Actaeon, he a hunter of animals suddenly and overwhelmingly engulfed by the animal in himself. Think of his great antlered head looking down from his chimney breast at his cousin Antigone.

Think of Oedipus: the fins they have evolved from have outcropped in his feet, and that is what has lamed him.

The fin in the feet with which we walk to the Bastille, the fin in the hand with which we write the Communist Manifesto, that is the shadow that tracks our flight of fire.

In an intuitive way, Greek myth is on Haechel's side. As European history repeatedly is.

The authors and executors of the French Revolution dismantled a socio-political ancien regime. But what of our inner phylogenetic ancien regime? What of what outcropped in the Minotaur? Quite simply, it took over and ran the show, as it did later in revolutionary Russia.

Will the Minotaur sing our Marseillaise with us?

Will Nebuchadnezzar regressed sing our Hymn of Joy with us?

In his efforts to describe the enormities of the spermwhale, Ishmael called out, give me a condor's quill for a writing pen and Mount Vesuvius for an inkpot.

Similarly, when we come to write our revolutionary handouts, shouldn't we, remembering guillotine and Gulag, write them with an eagle quill moulted by Nebuchdnezzar, he who was King of Kings and Lord of Lords but who also, regressed to all-fours, did eat grass as oxen.

While what Conrad says implies the possibility of such regression he doesn't overtly talk about it. He talks rather about demonic possession. Not so much that. More alarmingly still, he talks about a man, a citizen of Brussels, who became a devil.

A modern European, heir to successive enlightenments, no fool, and yet, there he very visibly is, believing in powers of darkness, in demonic agencies, in devils, in human devils, in devils in human form – how can this cultural throwback be anything but a scandal?

The question is : how anomalous is he to Europe in recent times?

In these same recent times we are in the habit of saying that evil is banal. The choice Sophie is forced to make isn't however banal. Not to her, not to her children.

If nothing else, recent European history is both an opportunity and a demand to estimate ourselves anew.

One thing is sure: we will repeat history if we continue to make history on and from the assumptions of an inadequate anthropology.

Turning into Old Compton Street in the dream, we graduated from an anthropic to a deinanthropic experience of ourselves. But how secure are we in this graduation?

Are we fooling ourselves in thinking that it is a graduation? Samuel Beckett has said that progress is in depth. Have we in this dream progressed in depth? Can we, by consciously re-enacting it, habituate ourselves to all that we are below the repressing grid? The grid gone up, can we live from the roots of who we are? Can we devise a culture that will enable us to flourish from the roots of who we are?

Are such hopes delusions? One thing is sure: any part of the human psyche that isn't coming with us isn't behind us, it is ahead of us, waiting to trip us up. Boehme again:

In man is all whatsoever the sun shines upon or
heaven contains , also hell and all the deeps.

How can we legislate for such a being? How can such a being not be at odds with culture, no matter how hospitable? What hearing if any will the hell in us give to Pericles and Pico? What hearing if any will the deeps in us give to the Beatitudes?

Be it our smell brain or our reptile brain, is there in us something that will always be recalcitrant to culture?
Speaking to him out of a whirlwind, the answer his God guided Job to is, yes:

Canst thou draw out Leviathan with an hook? or his tongue with a cord which thou lettest down? Canst thou put an hook into his nose? or bore his jaw through with a thorn? Will he make many supplications unto thee? Will he make a covenant with thee? Wilt thou take him for a servant forever? Wilt thou play with him as with a bird? or wilt thou bind him for thy maidens? Shall the companions make a banquet of him? Shall they part him among the merchants? Canst thou fill his skin with barbed irons? or his head with fish spears? Lay thine hand upon him, remember the battle, do no more. Behold, the hope of him is in vain...

The hope of Leviathan in vain. And the inwardness that outcropped in the Minotaur and that engulfed Actaeon, the hope of that in vain.   And this God's answer to a man who has been broken down into his deinanthropic enormities, a man who, in the course of his forced disintegration into deinanthropus, cries out:

When I say my bed shall comfort me, my couch shall ease my complaint, then thou scarest me with dreams and terrifiest me through visions, so that my soul chooseth strangling and death rather than my life.

A spirit passed before my face and the hair of my flesh stood up.

Hell is naked before me and destruction hath no covering.

I am a brother to dragons and a companion to owls.

Only to be told in the end that his reptile brain will not sing his Psalms of Ascent with him.

What then of the dream ?
Dare we believe that it has found a way for us ?
Dare we believe that, although it will threaten to engulf us, our reptile brain is in the end amenable to amelioration ?   Look at it, how shy it is, how harmless it is, going about it's business among reeds at the edge of our oldest psychic sea. Hindus assure us that below what is oldest in us is what is immortal in us, is what is eternal in us.
What is immortal in us they call atman, what is eternal in us they call Brahman. Going further, they assure us that Atman is Brahman, Brahman being the Eternal Divine that grounds all things. It grounds them not just by being floor to them. It grounds them everywhich way, from above, from below, from within, from without.   All that we are, wherever we are, however we are, it grounds.

So there we have it - - - - the humanism of turning into Old Compton Street and walking along it with a karmic digging fork in our hand.

The humanism of letting our nature happen to us.

The humanism of living, of flourishing, from Eternal Brahman in us.

The humanism of being willing to let our humanity dissolve into Eternal Brahman in us.

Meister Eckhart describes this final transition:

Comes then the soul into the unclouded light of God. It is transported so far from creaturehood into nothingness that, of its own powers, it can never return to its senses and faculties or its former creaturehood. Once there, God shelters the soul's nothingness with his uncreated essence, safeguarding it's creaturely existence. The soul has dared to become nothing, and cannot pass from its own being into nothingness and back again, losing its own identity in the process, except God safeguarded it. This must needs be so.

Now again, this time in fancy, I travel by train with Lorna and Sara, my godchildren, to a dinosaur exhibition in the zoo in Dublin. I am happy for them to come back and find me in the Cretaceous, to lead me forward through thirty million years into the Jurassic, all the way in to where he red-roaringly stands, the Tyrant himself, tall enough to look in at them asleep in their first-floor bedroom back in Connemara.

Coming home in the train, in a continuing fancy, I look at them, at Sara and Lorna, across a Mesozoic savannah, and I wonder both ways: what if the dream lied ? but, altogether more challengingly, what if it didn't ?

What if humanity is possible ?

Taking in a yet deeper breath of Jurassic air, I ask

What if humanity is deinanthropically possible ?

What if we can be who we are,

Deinanthropus ?

Assuming that we can be , it is , I believe, a desirable ambition only within the providential care of a religion great enough to meet our need. That Christianity can be as great as we would deinanthropically need it to be I have no doubt. Let me say why.

To be deinanthropus is to be natively and almost infinitely available to immanence. It is to be natively and almost infinitely available to transcendence.

Now I speak of Jesus.

From the moment he crossed the Torrent, Jesus lived and was lived by this double availability as one simultaneous availability. Moreover, it was consciously, as microcosm, in Boehme's sense, that he lived and was lived by it. Saying the least we can say about this, it is the next big event in the evolution of our planet since the origin of DNA. And I can imagine nothing better for ourselves as we microcosmically are and for the earth in all its geological ages, past and to come, than that it would become encoded as a permanent evolutionary attainment in our DNA. A hope not so fantastic as it would at first sight seem when we think that metamorphosis has become genetically encoded in insects. Relevant here is something J.B.S.Haldane has said:

It is my suspicion that the universe isn't only
queerer than we suppose, it is queerer than we
can suppose.

Queer and improbable things can happen in it and to it. But, be that as it may.

Coming back from the liberalities of science fiction, there he is, Gerald Manley Hopkins telling us that man is no-man-fathomed man.

Listening to the Passion narratives, as Holderlin listened to Sophoclean tragedy, I think I hear, I am sure I hear, that man, in the gender inclusive sense, is being man-fathomed. A Christian, I think I hear, I am sure I hear, that man is being redemptively Godman-fathomed.

Let us look at ourselves.

Let us look at

Godman-fathomed humanity

Let us look at a wonder neither seen nor foreseen by the prophets and sybils of the Sistine ceiling, neither seen nor foreseen therefore by Renaissance humanism -let us look at

Deinanthropus

In the beginning, Goethe said, was the deed.

What Jesus undertook to do and undergo is, I believe, an originating deed. Given a chance, and with our good will, it would, I believe, generate a culture that would accommodate us as we have never previously been accommodated.

Wouldn't only accommodate us as an accomplished ontological fact of course.

Would religiously and ritually accommodate us all the way into our further and final evolution.

IN PROSPECT

Today in Killarney I passed a very red butcher's shop and later, in another street, I passed a dentist's surgery, and I thought of that moment in the Precambrian, lasting millions of years of course, when a micro-organism abandoned photosynthesis as a way of obtaining energy for itself and turned to meat-eating. Three hundred million years later his continuously impromptu mouth had become the fiercely fixed mouth of tyrannosaurus rex and a hundred million years further along, two sounds, one of a meat cleaver on a chopping block, the other a dentist's drill. Something else that didn't happen might have happened. Looking through a restaurant window I might have seen someone, with civilized table manners, eating a blood pudding, that, mixed with other things, the blood of a pig in a pig's scraped intestine. Right then and there I wanted to annul the Precambrian moment in me. Threatening the livelihood of butcher and dentist, I wanted to shed the instinctive spearing savagery, now the mass-murderous, slaughterhouse savagery, that they are so rooted in. Civilized though I am, they are rooted in me, all my talk about the Good, the True and the Beautiful phonetically favoured by them. Similarly favoured, when I sing them, are the quavers and crotchets of my everlasting love for the woman I love:

> Till all the seas gang dry, my dear,
> And the rocks melt with the sun,
> Oh I will love thee still, my dear,
> While the sands of time shall run.

It is the old, sad recognition: teeth bet the Beatitudes to a place in my head. It is through the incisors of a carnivore that I speak them:

> Blessed are the poor in spirit: for theirs is the kingdom of heaven.
> Blessed are they that mourn: for they shall be comforted.
> Blessed are the meek: for they shall inherit the earth.
> Blessed are they that do hunger and thirst after righteousness: for they
>   shall be filled.
> Blessed are the merciful: for they shall obtain mercy.
> Blessed are the pure in heart: for they shall see God.
> Blessed are the peacemakers: for they shall be called the children of God.
> Blessed are they which are persecuted for righteousness' sake: for theirs

is the kingdom of heaven.
   Blessed are ye, when men shall revile you, and persecute you, and shall
      say all manner of evil against you, for my sake. Rejoice and be
   exceedingly glad, for great is your reward in heaven.

Making lurid the fact, making morally hectic the fact, that meat-eating is
anatomically, physiologically, metabolically, instinctively and emotionally built
into us. Supporting it a drive to turn destructively upon all forms of life and,
yet more terrible, this drive to destruction has invaded and, in extreme cases,
has come to occupy other drives, including the drive to self-reproduction. Men
confess to sexual arousal in the course of killing. A woman has confessed to
having an orgasm in the course of axing her former lover. The sexually speared
bison bull and the sexually aroused birdman depicted in the pit in Lascaux
witness to an impulse so factually fantastic that it shouldn't surprise us if the
very elements we are made of walked out on us.

      O Peggy Gordon, you are my darlin,
      Come sit you down upon my knee;
      Come tell to me the very reason
      Why I am slighted so by thee

Christian theologians of Roman Catholic persuasion insist that there is a
natural moral law.
   But what if in its dealings with itself and with us nature is at once
unthinking and conscienceless? What if it is only in emancipation from nature
that I do not turn in at the butcher's door, that I do not fall in with the
Precambrian transition to meat-eating?
   Meat-eating and the entirely wretched impulse depicted in the Palaeolithic
pit are but instances, two among a multitude of natural inclinations that leave
me as genetically self-contradicted as the bison bull now is, he having a spear in
his phallus, he having an impulse to destruction at the heart of his impulse to
creation.

      I was three shadows in one man;
      One shadow shaved a Piltdown jaw;
      Though my fingers made a Decalogue
      My fists fulfilled the law
      That gave dark streets dictatorship:
      Not just that or this,

> Everything fell from its God-given form
> For adultery with the abyss.

And Norse myth tells us that, insecurely chained up in every gene, is a wolfish impulse to ragnarok. That too is what the mural in the pit of our being is so luridly telling us.

Jesus bleeds with our bleeding planet. In that he receives the Palaeolithic bleeding lance into himself, he bleeds redemptively with it. And, in that he was willing to be the victim in a last supper, he annulled that first Precambrian supper, giving our planet an alternative evolutionary future.

From its first supper to its last supper ours was a red planet. It would therefore be wonderful if we could say that, wholly effective in its first enactment, we do not need to turn in daily or ever again at the door of the house of the Last Supper. But Jesus did say, "do this in memory of me". Would it be impious to plead with him to release us form this obligation? It isn't lightly that I ask this question. I do so because I believe that Christianity is in trouble in its central ritual. Collectively, verses 48 to 58 of chapter six of St. John's Gospel, are indeed a hard saying:

> I am the bread of life. Your fathers did eat manna in the wilderness, and are dead. This is the bread which cometh down from heaven, that a man may eat thereof, and not die. I am the living bread which came down from heaven: if any man eat of this bread, he shall live forever: and the bread that I will give is my flesh, which I will give for the life of the world.
> The Jews therefore strove among themselves, saying, how can this man give us his flesh to eat?
> Then Jesus said unto them, verily, verily, I say unto you, except ye eat the flesh of the Son of man, and drink his blood, ye have no life in you. Who so eateth my flesh and drinketh my blood, hath eternal life; and I will raise him up at the last day. For my flesh is meat indeed, and my blood is drink indeed. He that eateth my flesh, and drinketh my blood, dwelleth in me and I in him. As the living Father hath sent me, and I live by the Father: so he that eateth me, even he shall live by me. This is that bread which came down from heaven: not as your fathers did eat manna, and are dead: he that eateth of this bread shall live for ever. These things said he in the synagogue as he taught in Capernaum. Many therefore of his disciples, when they heard this, said, this is a hard saying:

who can bear it?

In SLÍ na FÍRINNE, therefore, we hope that it is with Christ's blessing that we will migrate from the Mass to Ephphatha, that the ritual of opening our eyes and minds, and to Tenebrae, that the ritual of closing our eyes and going beyond mind.

And if we are wrong in this, our plea is that God will accept us in our wrongness.

As we see it, God's redemption is actively immanent in the world. This means that we can think of the Eucharist in the broader sense of eucharistic reception. As such it doesn't need to be carnivorous. It can occur by many means and in many modes. I can eucharistically receive my salvation in the simple sacramental act of sacramentally listening to a river.

Eucharistic reception can be by means of any one of my five senses. In thanksgiving to God in Christ, it can be by means of inhaling the fragrance of wild woodbine or feeling my hand growing cold in winter river-water.

The challenge now is to annul the Precambrian moment in us and to fall in with the Earth's alternative evolutionary future.

Bright Angel Trail, as Jesus pioneered it, is open before us.

In prospect, coming up over its own karmic horizon,

is

Gaiakhty

is

Buddh Gaia

We are talking about a Christian departure from Last Supper Christianity to Karmic Canyon Christianity, from Jesus sharing self-sacrificial bread and wine with his disciples to Jesus doing and undergoing immensities under all earthly and psychic seafloors, the immensity of chalicing his finfraught hands down into the mirroring rockpool and, from a nunatak at Hakatai height within the Canyon, the immensity of looking down into and inheriting his own and Adam's empty skull, these the conditions in which he was wholly available to God, in karmic completion available, in utter emptiness available.

It is time to add a chapter to The Origin of Species. Come to think of it, a coda of one short paragraph will do. It will say that in consequence of two great deeds undertaken and carried through in the course of two days and two nights in the Karmic Canyon a new species has come into existence. It will say that from its beginnings all over again the Earth is now a new evolutionary story. It is Buddh Gaia, it will say, all the way forward from its nebular beginnings.

Let us become and let us be what we are, a new species, our newness maintained and promoted by two rituals.

BRIGHT ANGEL TRAIL

In a letter written by him to the abbot of St-Thierry, St. Bernard objects to what for him is an extravagance of costly and distracting ornamentation in churches. That done, he goes on to mock what for him are the merely fantastical, sculpted bestiaries of the monastic cloister:

> But in the cloister, under the eyes of the Brethern who read there, what profit is there in those ridiculous monsters, in that marvellous and deformed comeliness, that comely deformity? To what purpose are those unclean apes, those fierce lions, those monstrous centaurs, those half-men, those striped tigers, those fighting knights, those hunters winding their horns? Many bodies are there seen under one head, or again, many heads to a single body. Here is a four-footed beast with a serpent's tail; there, a fish with a beast's head. Here again the forepart of a horse trails half a goat behind it, or a horned beast bears the hinder quarters of a horse. In short, so many and so marvellous are the varieties of divers shapes on every hand, that we are more tempted to read in the marble than in our books, and to spend the whole day in wondering at these things rather than in meditating the law of God. For God's sake, if men are not ashamed of these follies, why at least do they not shrink from the expense?

The man who preached a crusade against Muslims here preaching a crusade against humanity, against all of us in our phylogenetic humanity.
phylogenetic we are. Hybrid in anatomy and instinct we are. A fish with the head of a beast we are. Cerebrally high-browed and low-browed and browless we are. Ibis-headed like the Egyptian god Thoth we are. Ram-headed like the Egyptian Sungod at evening we are, falcon-headed like that same god in the morning we are. Centaurs we are. Minotaurs we are. Boumorphic in our bovine desire to be bull-mounted we are.

There is all Africa and her prodigies in us.

I have discovered for myself that the old human and animal life, indeed the entire prehistory and past of all sentient being, works on, loves on, hates on, thinks on in me.

The mind of man is capable of anything – because everything is in it, all the past as well as all the future.

Try as St. Bernard may to keep his Citeaux doors closed against it, the Jurassic, already always within, will insist on its dues, will insist on its ancient phylogenetic ground rent.

Try as he may to ensure otherwise, St. Bernard's unadorned, undistracting, plain columns in church and cloister will burgeon into totem poles.

Better therefore to seek the sanctity not of exclusion and repression but of inclusion and integration. This, after all, is what Jesus had in mind when he cupped his fin-fraught hands down into the mirroring rockpool on the floor of the Karmic Canyon.

In Slí na Fírinne, therefore, our four minarets will be four totem poles, all that we phylogenetetically have been and are climbing up spirally, in high relief, around them.

That the same thing as Bright Angel Trail climbing up around them.

HE DESCENDED INTO HELL

How shockingly new Jesus is!

Heaven-holiness we have heard of and some there are who credit it.

In Jesus, in Gethsemane, and in hell itself, holiness extended its range.

Shockingly, Jesus is hell-holiness, and that is troublesome Good News for all religions, not just for Christianity.

In Gethsemane, it was from within the Minotauric condition, suffering it, that Jesus redeemed it, living it wholly and holily up out of that last chasm of the Labyrinth. Similarly in hell. It was from within perdition, suffering it, that he redeemed it, living it wholly and holily up into a condition not yet known to Beatrice.

The vast and stupendous error of Michelangelo's painted gable is that perdition is shown to be an act of divine damnation, Christ himself, all too immensely and wilfully, its earthquaking agent. Here, in spectacular display, is a betrayal of Christ out of all proportion to his betrayal by Judas.

No, hell isn't God's doing. Perdition isn't damnation. God doesn't damn. We think more truly when we think of it this way: in consequence of his will and ambition to equality with God an abyss opened and yawned within Lucifer and, still feeding and feeding off his pride, he sank down, down, forever down into it.

Something similar, if not so immense, happened to Adam and Eve.

Remedially relevant here is a poem D.H. Lawrence wrote late in his life:

It is not easy to fall out of the hands of the living God:
They are so large, and they cradle so much of a man.
It is a long time before a man can get himself away.
Even through the greatest blasphemies, the hands of the living God
Will continue to cradle him.

And still through knowledge and will, he can break away,
man can break away, and fall from the hands of God
into himself alone, down the godless plunge of the abyss,
a god-lost creature turning upon himself
in the long, long fall, revolving upon himself
in the endless writhe of the last, the last self-knowledge
which he can never reach till he touch the bottom of the abyss
which he can never touch, for the abyss is bottomless.
And there is nothing else, throughout time and eternity

but the abyss, which is bottomless,
and the fall to extinction, which can never come,
for the abyss is bottomless,
and the turning plunge of writing of self-knowledge, self-
    analysis
which goes further and further, and yet never finds an end
For there is no end,
It is the abyss of the immortality
Of those that have fallen from God.

Jesus wasn't only content to be born on the bestial floor, that a prognostication of his agony in the garden. In unreserved com-passion with spirits and souls that have fallen into the immortality of their falleness from God, the abyss that opened in Lucifer opened in him, and down, down he willingly sank, forever down into bottomless perdition.

The Buddha also, it is said, went down into hell, he to roar as a sugata lion roars, this in the hope of awakening suffering souls all the way back along the eight-fold chain of causation, into final release from the weary wheel of existence. And it would of course be good, in the sense of aiding them, to imagine that lion roar traversing all worlds, not just the hell-world.

Going further than the Buddha, or was it Avalokiteshvara, Jesus took hell upon himself. He became perdition. In William Law's phrase, he became a Principle of Heavenly Life within it and in this way redeemed it, or, as the inn-keepers and cooks of medieval Chester would have it, in this way he harrowed it. No, Jesus doesn't earthquake souls down into hell. Shockingly, he re-emerges among us as hell-holiness and so, the next time a gable becomes available to us, that is what we should have it say to us.

Jesus didn't only pioneer a way for all things. Wherever it is called for, and it isn't only in hell that it is called for, he is a redeemer not in the sense of buying someone back out of slavery but in the sense of suffering our way for us. In this regard, what we must remember about Jesus is that in the Canyon as well as in hell he worked at a depth where 'I' is 'We', where the singular is plural, where the one is all, and this is why it isn't fantastical to talk about

                    Gaiakhty

        about

                    Buddh Gaia

an altogether surer outcome, coming as it does from below, than the new heaven and the new earth that early Christians lived in imminent expectation of.

HOMING INSTINCT

Unlike the Calvary cross the Golgotha cross is not made of timber. Emanating from within us, as an instinct hitherto dormant would, it is a willingness in co-operation with God's grace to ascend in serial self-abnegation to what, in first exposure to it, will seem like a godless summit:

N
A
D
A
Y EN EL MONTE NADA
N
A
D
A

N
A
D
A

N
A
D
A

We are talking here about the awakening in us of a homing instinct and, as the further flourishing of the reproductive instinct at puberty does, it tends to monopolise us to its sole and single purpose. To the extent that we yield to it, it reorientates us to a destination outside the universe and outside ourselves, to reimmersion in God.

Going with it, we must learn to fly light. Not just in the sense that our bones must become as light as the bones of birds. Not without a furious fight-back on its part, we must learn to forgo, to let go, all sense of self, until in the end we are as consciously void of it awake as we are unconsciously void of it in dreamless sleep, and now, like a seagull in an updraught of air above an island at sea, our soaring is effortless.

Strange to say, it all begins where it began for Jesus, in a depth many Palaeozoic seafloors beneath the still inexpert flight of archaeornis. There, as Jesus did, we begin to be heavy with all that we karmically have been and are.

It isn't at all a trivial question: how many lives, incarnate and discarnate, will we be engulfed by before our homing instinct awakens unassuagably in us?

It awakened, a little politely we feel, in Henry Vaughan:

> O how I long to travel back,
> And tread again that ancient track!
> That I might once more reach that plain
> Where first I left my glorious train;
> From whence th'enlightened spirit sees
> That shady City of Palm-trees.
> But ah! my soul with too much stay
> Is drunk, and staggers in the way!
> Some men a forward motion love,
> But I by backward steps would move;
> And when this dust falls to the urn,
> In that state I came, return.

Noticeable in this piece is that, while he foresees physical death, Vaughan doesn't so much as allude to mystical death. Destination for him is continuing personal existence, jubilant everlastingly, in the celestial city.

To die mystically is to return not in the state we came but as we were before we were, innocent of ex-sistence, our wilful alienation from God within God.

Famously, Plotinus described our return as a flight of the alone to the Alone.

In an evolutionary sense, we are the new archaeornis or, more appropriately perhaps, we are the new eo-ornis, the new dawn-bird.

It's the teleological shadow we cast all the way down into the Canyon:

N

A

D

A

Y EN EL MONTE NADA

N

A

D

A

N

A

D

A

N

A

D

A

It is the teleological shadow that awakens in trilobite and ammonite, giving them the wings for their

HOMECOMING

Tenebrae

The Ritual

of

Our Further

and

Final Evolution

Pascal draws attention to "the difference between a book accepted by a people and a book that creates a people".

We believe that in Tenebrae we have a ritual that is adequate to all that we deinanthropically are. We believe that, mediating the necessary graces to us, it can enable us into and through our further and final evolution.

Oh dichosa ventura

What is being proposed is this: much as nature has naturally selected metamorphosis in insects so should religion religiously select the most mystical of rituals. On the assumption that there is more to nature than Darwin saw in it and more to genetics than Mendel saw in it, it could be that what religion selects nature will in time select. Having become second nature, habit might in time become primary nature.

I

Having crossed the Torrent, Jesus goes forward in a double progress.

In the first, setting out as Lamb of God, he goes forward through the Garden of Olives and Calvary, and, hell harrowed, he re-emerges in the Garden of the Sepulchre.

In the second, seeking to pioneer the mystical way, not just for himself but for all things, he goes forward as microcosm into Gethsemane, on to Golgotha, and, Ordovician desert dust in his hair, he comes back and, in all the world, there is neither bush nor star that isn't surprised by what has happened to it.

In the second progress, occurring simultaneously with the first, Golgotha is the place of the skull, not also like Calvary, the place of a timber cross. It is the place not of physical but of mystical death, a dying so total that we are able in the end to say what Tauler said:

NON SUM

to sing as Eckhart sings:

Oh, wonder of wonders, when I think of the union the soul has with God! He makes the enraptured soul to flee out of herself, for she is no more satisfied with anything that can be named. The spring of Divine Love flows out of the soul, and draws her out of herself into the unnamed Being, into her first source, which is God alone.

II

As we ascend the Hill of the Skull, the skull a nunatak rising above dualizing consciousness, we learn not to project the horrid but holy enormities of Calvary on to it. Such as they are, the enormities of Calvary are different in kind from the enormities of Golgotha. For far too long our awareness of Christ in the Garden of Olives has eclipsed our awareness of Christ in Gethsemane. Also, our awareness of Christ on Calvary has eclipsed our awareness of Christ on Golgotha. The emergence of Gethsemane from its eclipse by the Garden of Olives and the emergence of Golgotha from its eclipse by Calvary is the emergence of Christianity into full, mystical maturity, and the ritual that best expresses that maturity is Tenebrae.

Coming to it, Jesus and his disciples cross a stream called the Kedron.

To Jesus alone, as he crosses it, it seems as deep as a summit it mirrors. More.

It is as deep as the single star it mirrors is high.

Sensing enormities, his disciples hesitate.

Not for the reason that they have more nerve than the others, Jesus invites Peter, James and John to continue forward with him. This they do but only as far as the borders of a land that falls so precipitously away from itself that you would think, looking over the rim, that it wanted to fall out of the universe altogether. The thing too much for them, they take refuge in sleep.

A dip in your road, the Angel of the Trail says. Go down into it and it will get to you. Even if your mind was as small and as sure of its sanity as the mind of a beetle is, it will get to you.

Knowing that his hour is upon him, Jesus consents to engulfment.

By nightfall he is contemporary with sea scorpions and ammonites.

By midnight, a Precambrian moon lighting his way, he is sixty million years below the first jelly fish, below the first alga colonies.

Looking up, having reached the end of his descent, he imagines he can see them, pterosaurs flying in Mesozoic skies, and plesiosaurs and ichthyosaurs swimming in Mesozoic seas, two thousand million years above him.

ANTIPHONS

V. In man is all whatsoever the sun shines upon and heaven contains.

R Also hell and all the deeps.

V. O the mind, mind has mountains, cliffs of fall frightful, sheer, no-man-fathomed.

R Hold them cheap may who ne'er hung there.

V. The mind of man is capable of anything – because everything is in it:

R All the past as well as all the future.

The Angel points to a rockpool that mirrors the Orion-high karma of the ages. The risk hallucinating itself before him, Jesus pleads with God saying, what happened to Nebuchadnezzar can happen to me:

The same hour was the thing fulfilled upon Nebuchadnezzar: and he was driven from men, and did eat grass as oxen, and his body was wet with the dew of heaven, till his hairs were grown like eagles' feathers, and his nails like birds' claws.

128

What will happen to Idumea, he pleads, can happen to me:

The cormorant and the bittern shall possess it; the owl also and the raven shall dwell in it … and thorns shall come up in her palaces, nettles and brambles in the fortresses thereof: and it shall be an habitation of dragons, and a court for owls. The wild beasts of the desert shall also meet with the wild beasts of the island, and the satyr shall cry to his fellow: the screech owl also shall rest there, and find for herself a place of rest. There shall the great owl make her nest, and lay, and hatch, and gather under her shadow: there shall the vultures also be gathered, everyone with her mate.

ANTIPHONS

V. Fearfulness and trembling are come upon me.

R And horror has overwhelmed me.

V. I am a brother to dragons.

R I am a companion to owls.

V. I am all broken in the place of dragons.

R I am covered in the shadow of death.

LECTIO:

Haechel, a German biologist of the nineteenth century, advanced the idea that evolution recapitulates itself in us.

To put it crudely: in the course of our embryonic development we are protiston, we are fish, we are amphibian, we are reptile, we are mammal, we are primate, and finally, we are human. It is an idea which suggests that we go back a long way, back indeed to where we find ourselves now, here with Jesus on the floor of the Palaeozoic. Discredited for good scientific reasons, it is nonetheless an idea that makes alarming if ad hoc sense to many of us in immediate experience. We only have to think of Nietzsche who says:

I have discovered for myself that the old human and animal life, indeed the entire prehistory and past of all sentient being, works on, loves on, hates on, thinks on, in me.

There are nightmares we awaken from. There are nightmares we wake up into. Here we are waking up to the ominously flourishing fact that we aren't what the Bible says we are, a special creation, unique to ourselves, high and dry above animals and, in intellect, just below angels. Here we are suffering a descent into nature, into modern nature and downwards from there into Mesozoic and Palaeozoic nature. Yet more alarming is the fact that the Jurassic I sink down into isn't only outside me, around me, it is in me, actively.

Putting a Jurassic tooth in it, Nietzsche is saying that Tyrannosaurus Rex thinks in me.

Modern man that I am, I am nonetheless Ordovician.

Cultivated man I am, and yet the reptile brain, the brain of a crocodile, is alive and well in me.

We are awakening to nightmare.

And that awakening – it is the chalice the Angel is offering to Jesus.

There are nights when we will be tempted to believe that just as there is a physical appendix so is there a karmic appendix. Boiled by the purifying fires, it bursts, and so flooded are we now with archaic miasma that we only have to do what Jesus did, we only have to put our hand to our brow, and there it is.

It is introspectively to night that we are palaeontologists.

ANTIPHONS

V. You make us to see hard things about ourselves, O Lord,

R You make us to drink the wine of astonishment.

V. The cup of trembling you make us to drink, O Lord,

R The very dregs of it we drink

An Act of Faith:

> I can't sense you or know you or name you, God.
> I can't find you inside me or in the world outside.
> But wherever I am, and however I am, I am in your
> blissful safekeeping, God.
> Here on the floor of the Karmic Canyon, I am
>   in your blissful safekeeping, God.
> In heaven, in earth and in hell I am

    in your blissful safekeeping, God.
Yes, even in hell I am
    in your blissful safekeeping, God.

An Act of Confidence in God, in the God Who is in Christ.

Know ye not, St. Paul says,

> Know ye not that so many of us were baptized into Jesus Christ were
> baptized into his death. Therefore we are buried with him by baptism
> into death: that like as Christ was raised up from the dead by the glory
> of the Father, even so we also should walk in newness of life.

It is in sacramental, in particular it is in baptismal, assimilation to Jesus, the
Christ, that we would fare forward.

LECTIO:

They that do down to the sea in ships,
    that do business in great waters:
These see the works of the Lord
    and his wonders in the deep.
For he commandeth and raiseth the stormy wind
    which lifteth up the waves thereof.
They mount up to the heavens,
    they go down again to the depths,
Their soul is melted because of trouble.
They reel to and fro,
    and stagger like a drunken man,
    and are at their wits' end.
Then they cry unto the Lord in their trouble,
    And he bringeth them out of their distresses.
He maketh the storm a calm,
    so that the waves thereof are still.
Then are they glad because they be quiet;
    so that he bringeth them unto their desired haven.

Again, An Act of Faith:

The waters we do business in aren't only modern waters with stingrays and sharks and coelacanths and turtles and dolphins swimming in them. They are also Mesozoic waters with plesiosaurs and ichthyosaurs swimming in them, and with pterosaur shadows flying in them.

And it isn't only in outer waters that we do business.

When our inner Cretaceous or Triassic waters do business with us then indeed is our soul melted because of trouble, then indeed do we need the assurance of an assuring psalm:

> If I ascend up into heaven, thou art there;
> If I make my bed in hell, behold, thou are there.
> If I take the wings of the morning
>   and dwell in the uttermost parts of the sea,
>   even there shall thy hand lead me
>   and thy right hand hold me.
> If I say, surely the darkness shall cover me,
>   even the night shall be light to me.
> Yea, the darkness hideth not from Thee,
>   the night shineth as the day.
> The darkness and the light are both alike to Thee
> For Thou hast possessed me in my reins:
>   Thou hast covered me in my mother's womb.
> I will praise Thee,
>   for I am fearfully and wonderfully made.
> Marvellous are Thy works,
>   and that my soul knoweth right well.

God's own assurance we need to walk in:

> When thou passest through the waters, I will be with thee; and through the rivers, they will not overflow thee: when thou walkest through the fire, thou shalt not be burned; neither shall the flame kindle upon thee.

Assured, we continue awake.

God's assurance notwithstanding, here on the floor of the Karmic Canyon, pterosaurs flying in Mesozoic skies above him, Jesus is sore amazed. And he is heavy.

He is karmically heavy, almost to the point of going down on all fours, with all that we phylogenetically are.

Awakening to them, seeing the heavens and hells in us, seeing the precosmic deeps in us, he is sorrowful unto death.

In a hallucination of hope, he sees his psyche opening as the Red Sea did, and there he is, walking dryshod through between the perfectly accommodating, high canyon walls of it.

But no. Still there, showing no overt emotion, Bright Angel points to the mirroring rockpool.

Strata not in the Canyon are mirrored in it.

All time, past, present and to come, being psychologically synchronous in Jesus to night, a stratum rich in fossils of ourselves in our present precarious state of evolution is mirrored in it.

Unnervingly impassive, Bright Angel is challenging him to undergo our next evolutionary transition. To undergo it as microcosm, as the macrocosm in little. To be such a microcosm, to be it consciously, is at any time a deeply assailing terror. To be consciously a microcosm and to consciously consent to consciously undergo the disintegrations and reintegrations of our next evolutionary transition – well, we shouldn't wonder that even Jesus sweated blood at the very thought and prospect of it.

ANTIPHONS

V. The thing which I greatly feared is come upon me.

R And that which I was afraid of is come unto me.

V. I am counted with those that go down into the pit.

R I am gone down into the lowest pit, into darkness, into the depths.

V. Hell is naked before me.

R And Destruction has no covering.

V. My confidence is rooted out of me.

R I am come before the King of Terrors.

V. Truly my soul waits upon God.

R From him comes my salvation.

V. My soul, wait thou only upon God.

R For my expectation is from him.

LECTIO:

As for Jesus at this hour: conscious of himself as microcosm, he feels that he is at once older and younger than the stars in the Precambrian sky above him.
It almost quenchs him to think it, but to night, having put on perdition as he would a shirt, he thinks that astronomies of stars aren't at all as real as the astronomy of how he feels.

If a crocodile could become morally aware of himself, if he could become morally aware of his long-drawn-out, murderous mouth, if a conscience as acute as them emerged in his teeth – that, by way of entrance into his Passion, is how Jesus feels.
To night everything is re-estimated.
What, compared with moral awareness, are stars?

Still waiting beside it, Bright Angel points to the Rockpool .

Going to it, the shadow of a pterosaur upon him, Jesus cups his phylogenetically heavy hands down into it and when, having settled, the water in this improvised chalice mirrors the karma of the ages, piled Orion high above him, he drinks it.

Whether the universe staggers we do not know, but Jesus, its microcosm, most certainly does. But it could be that for once astrological influences work both ways, the microcosm in this instance having an effect on the macrocosm. The difference here is that it is deliberately as microcosm that Jesus does what he does.

For a while, which to Jesus himself seems like an eternity, it is touch and go. He might sink down to all-fours, as Nebuchadnezzar did, or, engulfed by his most primitive instincts, he might hear from within himself what he'd have heard in Idumea, screech owl calling to screech owl, a satyr crying to his fellow and, from their roosts, a vulture croaking to her mate.

Sigmund Freud expressed his highest hope for us in a short, single sentence: that where the id is ego shall be. In Idumea, which was once a well ordered city, simulacrum of a well ordered psyche, we have the terrifying, hair-raising opposite of this: where self and self-control used to be there is now a free-for-all of our most primitive instincts and impulses. Repression hasn't worked.

Jesus doesn't only awaken, as Nietzsche did, to all that we phylogenetically have been and are. In drinking the mirroring cup, he lets it all happen to him. In a sense, he lets evolution recapitulate itself in him, only now he lives it all towards God. Trilobite life he lives towards God. Horseshoe crab life he lives towards God. Sea scorpion life he lives towards God. Ichthyosauric life he lives towards God. Pterosauric life he lives towards God. Dinosauric life he lives towards God. The life of Tyrannosaurus Rex he lives towards God. Tiger life he lives towards God. Condor life, above the Andes, and above Guernica, he lives towards God. Colosseum life and Auschwitz life he lives towards God. The shadow of a pterosaur upon him, that shadow becoming consubstantial with him, Jesus lives all Canyon life in all its ages, he lives it towards and into and in God. And so it is that in all its ages and voices the Earth is now an oratorio. And now we know for sure that there has been astrological alteration. Where once we listened to the supernal music of the spheres, it is now for the spheres and for the near and the far stars to listen to the supernal music of the Earth.

How many such wonders are there in our galaxy?

In the universe, how many?

Are we known elsewhere in the universe for a light not of the physical spectrum that distinguishes our planet? Are we known for the single supernal note that distinguishes it?

And so, at the end of this our first night with Christ in the Canyon, it wouldn't be unduly unwise to say, yes, maybe we can be an evolutionary success.

ANTIPHONS

V. Angel, Bright Angel, Angel of the Trail.

R. Angel who, in a depth of the Canyon called Gethsemane,
  offers me the mirroring cup.

V. Angel who, on a height within the Canyon called Golgotha,
  offers me my own empty skull.

R. My own blessed fullness of being I drink from the cup.

V. My own blessed abeyance of being I drink from my own
  empty skull.

R. It is what Gethsemane means, blessed fullness of being

before God.

V. It is what Golgotha means, blessed abeyance of being
   into and in God.

Our transition to Golgotha is a prayer prayed without reservation in all that I am by all that I am, it is a prayer prayed beyond all longing to look back over my shoulder at my life in the world.

Let us pray:

> May I be as out of your way awake, God, as I am
>   in dreamless sleep.

And there it is,
>   Golgotha

Seeing its overhangs, and seeing how an insurgence of pride might well set off an avalanche that would carry me down into hell, into an abyss below hell, I make the sign of the cross on myself, saying:

It is in sacramental assimilation to Jesus, the Christ, who climbed this hill, that I would climb it. It is in the hope that I have been invited by God in Christ that I would climb it. In Christ is my invitation. In Christ's ascent is my ascent.

At every step in my ascent I am spoken to.

> O wretched condition of this life wherein it is so dangerous to live and so difficult to find the truth. That which is most clear and true is to us most obscure and doubtful and we therefore avoid it though it is most necessary for us. That which shines the most and dazzles our eyes, that we embrace and follow after though it is most hurtful to us and makes us stumble at every step. In what fear and danger then must man be living, seeing that the very light of his natural eyes by which he directs his steps is the very first to bewilder and deceive him when he would draw near unto God. If he wishes to be sure of the road he travels on he must close his eyes and walk in the dark if he is to journey in safety from his domestic foes, which are his own senses and faculties.

A first sip it is from my own empty skull. And how bitter to my accustomed sense and experience of myself it tastes. It tells me that the senses and the faculties with which I seek God eclipse God. It isn't a darkness in me that eclipses God. It is the light in me that does so.

ANTIPHONS

V. On Golgotha I come to know that it is because I am exile from God within God that I am in exile from God within God.

R It is of exile from God within God that I am constituted.

V. It is in cohering about a dualizing consciousness within God that I am exile from God.

R. In dualizing seeing, in dualizing hearing, in dualizing knowing, in dualizing consciousness of no matter what sort or kind, I am exile from God within God.

V. Experience of self and other-than-self is separation from God within God.

R On Golgotha it is by all that separates me from God within God that I am abandoned.

It is tough going.

It is only in moments of extravagant, desperate daring that I lie back in confidence into what God said to Julian of Norwich, into what, through her, he says to me:

Thou shalt not ben overcommen

Perdition outside God within God my address, I remember some lines from the Tao Te Ching:

The way out into the light often looks dark,
The way that goes ahead often looks as if it went back.

I remember that the Buddha talks not about the empty skull but about a mind whose elements have been dissolved.

And Chuang Tzu, he talks about a mind that has turned to ashes.

I remember a Sufi parable:

> There's a man walking home late at night. Turning into his own street, he walks past all the familiar doors, all the familiar small gardens. As he is approaching his own gate, he puts his hand in his waistcoat pocket to retrieve his key. To his great surprise it isn't in it. Nor is it in any other pocket. For a moment he is at a loss what to do. Ahead of him there is a street lamp shedding a very precise circle of light on the ground. Going forward into this circle, he walks round in it, seeking his key. After a while the local policeman comes along and asks him, what's up? "I'm searching for the key to my house", he replies. "I will help you" the policeman says. On all fours now, round and round they go, always careful to remain within the light. Frustrated, the policeman gives up and, coming to his feet, he asks with repressed annoyance, "are you sure you lost it here?" "Of course I didn't", the other says. "Where then did you lose it?" the policeman asks. "I lost it over there in that dark corner" the seeker, still seeking, replies. "So why aren't you searching there?" the openly annoyed policeman asks. "Because there is no light there", the seeker, secure in his circle, replies.

Seek for God as we may within the confining circle of sensory-intellectual light and the way to him will continue closed against us.

I remember a poem called The Hills by D.H. Lawrence:

> I lift up mine eyes unto the hills
> and there they are, but no strength comes from
> them to me.
> Only from darkness
> And ceasing to see
> Strength comes.

The ascent well known to him, St. John of the Cross lets us know what is up ahead of us:

> It is therefore very expedient and necessary, if the soul is to advance to these heights, that the dark night of contemplation should first bring it to nothing, and undo it in all its meannesses, bringing it into darkness, aridities, loneliness and emptiness; for the light that is to be given it is a certain divine light of the highest nature, surpassing all natural light, and

not naturally cognisable by the understanding. If the understanding is to be united with that light, and become divine in the state of perfection, it must first of all be purified and annihilated as to its natural light, which must be brought actually into darkness by means of this dim contemplation. This darkness must continue so long as it is necessary to destroy the habit, long ago contracted, of understanding things in a natural way, and until the divine enlightening shall have taken its place. And therefore, in as much as the power of understanding, previously exerted, is natural, the result is that the darkness now endured is awful, and most afflictive, as it were solid, because it reaches to, and is felt in, the innermost depths of the spirit.

Here, we are not talking about ordinary darkness, about darkness consequent upon the absence of light. Properly speaking, we are talking about Tenebrae, the very particular kind of mystical darkness that came so invasively down upon Jesus at noon on Good Friday. It is in the account of his Passion in Latin that we come upon the word:

Erat autem fere hora sexta, et tenebrae factae sunt in universam terram usque in horam nonam. Et obscuratus est sol: et velum templi scissum est medium.

And it was about the sixth hour and from then until the ninth hour there was darkness all over the earth, and the sun was darkened, and the veil in the temple was rent in the middle.

LECTIO:

Ordinary darkness is passive. There are nights when Tenebrae assails us. It assaults us. It builds to a tempest invading us in all that we are, making us aware of depths and roots in us that we previously had no inklings of. As Jonah was, we have as it were been heaved out over our conventional sense of ourselves and our destiny and we are now in the belly of the whale and the whale has gone down below the roots of the mountains, down into the precosmic abyss and, eternally lost there, we are being digested into precosmic anonymity.

And there are nights when this, our tenebration, goes hand in hand with our purification. Like a saucepan of milk left on a fire we come to the boil in all that we are and we boil over. Only no. It isn't a saucepan of milk, it is a witches cauldron of bad or even wicked karma that has accumulated over life-times, not all of them incarnations – that is what has come to the boil, it is boiling over, fogging our eyes and our minds from within, filling our room with the emerging moral pollution. So intense some nights is the purgatorial fire, we resign ourselves to not being there in the morning. Body and soul, instinct and intellect, we will have evaporated.

Sometimes we sense a love, a divine love, in the fire, and added to the anguish of it is the further anguish of our not being able to fully co-operate either with the fire or with the love, with the love-fire.

And there are torments. It is as if there is indeed a Great Adversary. By choice, he can become a King of Terrors, appearing as Death, as Bellial, as Sheol, as whatever takes his frightful fancy and there he is

    As

        Death's breakers closing in on me

    As

        Bellial's torrents ready to swallow me

    As

        Sheol's snares every side of me

    As

        Death's traps lying ahead of me

A Supreme Intelligence, he sees through us, and if there are hidden shames, he will put extreme, relentless and merciless pressure on us there. He having his way with us, we wont need to consult a dictionary to find out the meaning of the word 'torment'.

In all of this we are undergoing what St. John of the Cross calls the dark night of the soul. He calls it a hideous night, and yet, elsewhere he says this of it,

        Oh noche, que guiaste,
        Oh noche amable mas que el alborada.

        Oh night that guides,
        Oh night more lovely than dawn.

And he is right. Supremely hideous it is, and supremely lovely.

ANTIPHONS

V. In hearing and in seeing and in knowing I am the distance between me and God.

R As I experience myself awake, as I experience myself asleep, I am the distance between me and God.

V. On Golgotha it is by all that I am awake and asleep that I am abandoned.

R On Golgotha it is by al that separates me from God, including God as object of consciousness, that I am abandoned.

V. On Golgotha I experience myself not as my means of reaching God but as my continuing defense-works against God.

R On Golgotha I experience experience of self as separation.

It has been said: God always forgives, people sometimes forgive, nature never forgives.

As soon as it senses that its reign in us is threatened, nature fights back, furiously. With everything we are from the Precambrian till now it fights us and it doesn't work to do what a defeated wolf does. It doesn't work to roll over onto your back and expose your jugular. Do what we will, there will be nights when our instincts will let us know that we didn't know what it was we were letting ourselves in for when we crossed the Torrent. Even if no one laid a hand on him, Jesus would still look bruised. Whether on an igneous floor of it or on a Supai summit of it, Canyon work is Passion.

Out of what igneous extremity of Passion does Catherine of Siena speak when she says:

I have chosen suffering for my only consolation and I will gladly bear this and all other torments for the Saviour's sake for as long as it shall please his Majesty.

Out of what igneous extremity of Passion does St. Teresa of Avila speak when she says:

Thou seemest, Lord, to give severe tests to those who love Thee, but only that in the extremity of their trials they may learn the greater extremity of Thy love.

Christian bhaktas they are, and even when it involves them in tribulation, in dereliction, or in a descent into hell, their way to the summit is a way of love, and for them, no matter what, God is the Beloved. As he is indeed to St. John of the Cross, he also a Bhakta:

> Oh noche, que guiaste,
> Oh noche amable mas que el alborada:
> Oh noche que juntaste
> Amado con amada
> Amada en el Amado transformada.

Not only is the Dark Night a night that guides, it joins the lover and the Beloved and, yet more surprisingly, it transforms the lover into the Beloved.

Marguerite Porete speaks no less knowingly, no less nuptially, of Love:

> The soul now has no name but Union in Love. As the water that flows into the sea becomes sea, so does the soul become Love. Love and the soul are no longer two things but one.

Astonishingly, she talks about a next stage in our ascent.
A next stage? we ask. After Union in Love, a next stage?
Yes, she says, after Union in Love the next highest stage is the soul's fall from Love to nothingness.
A reminder that the path to the summit isn't single, isn't the same for all. Talking out of her own experience and being true to it, it is unlikely that St. Teresa of Avila for all her derelictions would say what Fenelon says:
God felt, God tasted and enjoyed is indeed God, but God with those gifts that flatter the soul. God in darkness, in privation, in forsakenness, in insensibility, is so much God, that He is so to speak God bare and alone.

For some, Golgotha, in Fenelon's derelictive description of it, isn't only in the offing. Already it overshadows them, forcing them to ascend in blind faith.

As reported by Plato, Socrates believed that it is in thinking immortal thoughts that we become immortal:

Now when a man abandons himself to his desires and ambitions, indulging them incontinently, all his thoughts of necessity become mortal, and as a consequence he must become entirely mortal, because he has nourished his mortal part. When on the contrary he has earnestly cultivated his love of knowledge and true wisdom, when he has primarily exercised his faculty to think immortal and divine things, he will – since in that manner he is touching the truth – become immortal of necessity, as far as it is possible for human nature to participate in immortality.

To which St. John of the Cross would say: if we are to prosper in our mystical ascent we must, setting foot on it, show ourselves willing to undergo tenebration not just in our lower faculties, those that concern themselves with mortal things, but also in our higher and highest faculties, those that concern themselves with immortal things:

> I say, then, that the soul, in order to be effectively guided to this state by faith, must not only be in darkness with respect to that part that concerns creatures and temporal things, which is the sensual and the lower part, but that likewise it must be blinded and darkened according to the part which has respect to God and to spiritual things, which is the rational and higher part …

A mahavakya of the Chandogya Upanishad is relevant here:

> Where nothing else is seen, nothing else is heard, nothing else is thought about, there's the Fullness.

as is a mahavakya of the Kena Upanishad

There goes neither the eye nor speech nor the mind: we know it not, nor do we know how to teach one about it. Different it is from all that is known and beyond the unknown it also is.

Jneyavarana is a word much in use among Mahayana Buddhists. It suggests that thinking and thoughts about it eclipse ultimate reality.

And when St. John of the Cross talks about our ascent in faith he is talking not about a rock of faith but about an abyss of faith, meaning that we are supported by nothing physical outside ourselves, by nothing mental or emotional inside ourselves, not by anything we can think or feel or know.

Jesus said, "the birds of the air have nests, foxes have holes, but the Son of Man has no where to lay his head". Ascending to Golgotha, the Place of the Skull, on Good Friday, he not only has no where outside his head on which to lay it, neither is there anything inside it on which he might lay it. No state of dreaming awareness, no state of waking awareness, no state of paranormal awareness. Nothing. "All strong rocks" Tauler says, "are broken here, all upon which the spirit might rest must be done away with". Which is what Mahayana Buddhists mean by niralambanavada, having as little support as we would in a void, that void within and without.

Especially as we ascend the Hill of the Skull of course, we should remember that nothingness means no-thing-ness not nihil.

Eckhart says sooth:

> Everything which has being hangs in the Naught. And that same naught is such an incomprehensible aught that all the spirits in heaven and upon earth can neither comprehend it nor sound it.

As mystics use them, the words emptiness, nothing, void, signify a mirum beyond being and non-being. And the best thing therefore that could happen to traditional metaphysics and physics is that they would become aware of their shortcomings, of their coming lamentably short.

Different it is from all that is known and beyond the unknown it also is.

This has vast and derelictive implications for us on our ascent.

ANTIPHONS

V. The birds of the air have nests, foxes have holes, but the Son of Man has nowhere to lay his head.

R. There is for me nowhere outside my head on which to lay my head.

V. There is for me nowhere inside my head on which to lay my head.

R. There is for me no state of waking awareness on which to lay my head.

V. There is for me no state of dreaming awareness on which to lay my head.

R. There is for me no state of dualizing consciousness, normal or paranormal, on which to lay my head.

Ascending, we climb up out of metaphysics into metanoesis.
Ascending, we climb up out of knowledge into gnosis.
Gnostically, we know that vision veils.
Gnostically, we know that the sempiternal rose doesn't bloom
in the Golgotha skull, and so, much as Beatrice took
over from Virgil so now must Bright Angel take over from
Beatrice.
Gnostically as we ascend we know that, conscious and unconscious, psyche is
the blind not the window.
Gnostically as we ascend we reluctantly come to know that, as well as being the
Metanoetic Nunatak, Golgotha is the Self-naughting Nunatak.

> Help me to be as out of your way awake, God, as I am
>   in dreamless sleep.

> Help me to be as out of your way awake, God, as I am
>   in dreamless sleep.

> Help me to be as out of your way awake, God, as I am
>   in dreamless sleep.

As there are earthquakes so are there mindquakes. Sooner or later as we ascend mind in us is mindquaked. In all that it is, in its senses and faculties, in its dreaming and in its waking, in all its states normal and paranormal, it is shifted to one side, and this is dereliction, woeful and dreadful beyond prior imagining. Now for sure has our rock of faith dissolved. Now for sure is our faith an abyss of faith, a void of faith, faith with nothing that we can sense or feel or imagine or know supporting it. Cataclysmically, in an instant perhaps, we have been made to learn that, in regard to our further ascent, mental activity is as little helpful to us as the activity of our spleen is. In stupendous dereliction we conclude that, in so far as seeing God is concerned, seeing veils.

Furthermore, the quaking to one side of the psyche is also a quaking of the psyche and so it is that all of our suppressed enormities emerge. Now we are compelled to credit the suggestion that we are a recapitulation of evolution. Nightmared enormously night after night we are many times broken down in our reluctance to believe that psyche is coextensive and cotemporal and in some sense consubstantial with the Canyon in all its strata. Karmically, the seabeds of the Canyon are the seabeds of the psyche. The Ordovician out there is the Ordovician in here. The Jurassic out there is the Jurassic in here.

The mind of man is capable of anything – because everything is in it, all the past as well as all the future.

Holy Thursday at night in Gethsemane and Good Friday at noon on Golgotha are a dark eternity of dread and terror, of dereliction and abandonment.
It is by our image of God and therefore by our expectation of felt assistance that we are abandoned. This a consequence of our having as it were been abandoned by our all to anthropomorpically creative, anthropomorphically projective, senses and faculties.
As though we had taken yet another sip from our own empty skull, we begin now to think of God as more like nothing than something, only as we have already indicated the nothing we here have in mind is anything but nihil. At the very thought of it, desire becomes longing and longing becomes yearning. Sensing it not with our senses, not with anything we are or could possibly be, the sense of it we do come to have has swoonings in it. To get to it we are willing to leave our very ability to experience it at home. Me as experiencer I leave at home. To be an experiencer implies the duality of the one experiencing and the thing experienced, and such duality is impediment and hurt to us now. It is this, our dualizing consciousness, that has been earthquaked to one side. Now in our yearning for God who is as far beyond nothing as he is beyond something, we practice the self-abeyance of dreamless sleep. In dreamless sleep we are unconsciously self-abeyant. Here on our Good Friday ascent we are consciously self-abeyant. Here I practice being as self-absent awake as I am in dreamless sleep.

ANTIPHONS

V. Our addiction to being ourselves is our addiction to our separation from God within God.

R. It is when it is under sustained and assailing threat as it is in Tenebration that we come to know how profound and various is our addiction to being individuals who, as such, exclude God within God.

V. Entering dreamless sleep, I unconsciously lose my addiction to being me. Entering God, I consciously lose my addiction to being me.

R. Seeking you, God, I seek to be as self-abeyant awake as I am in dreamless sleep.

V. Crossing into dreamless sleep, void of a sense of self as I then am, I do not say:

into your safekeeping I commend my self of being a self in its self-abeyance.

R. Seeking to cross into God from within God, I say it: into your safekeeping, God, I commend my sense of being a self in its self-abeyance, you having achieved this abeyance for me.

The Hill of the Skull is the Hill of Complete Kenosis.
The Mahayana Buddhist word for complete kenosis is svabhavasunyata, meaning emptiness in and of self-nature.
Little wonder that Peter, James and John have taken refuge in sleep. And little wonder that the precedent they set soon became a common practice.

> O the mind, mind has mountains, cliffs of fall
> Frightful, sheer, no-man-fathomed. Hold them cheap
> May who ne'er hung there …

Given how fathomlessly precipitous we inwardly are, it makes sense to not ask too much of ourselves.

Christ's invitation to us to watch with him, to stay awake with him, is no small matter. We are talking about being sym-pathetic with him, about being com-passionate with him, in his Progress back into universal at-one-ment not just with but in God. And so, while it isn't blameworthy to fall asleep on Jesus, he himself sore-amazed and wanting out, it is an adventure like no other to stay awake with him. A sip from the karmic cup, improvised from our fin-fraught hands, and a self-naughting sip from our own empty skull – first sips though they are, they quakingly forewarn us concerning what it is we are letting ourselves in for.

> And he went a little further, and fell on his face, and prayed, saying, O my Father, if it be possible, let this cup pass from me: nevertheless not as I will but as thou wilt.

Enormities like nothing before or since they are, the descent to the cup and the ascent to the skull.
And here we are, presuming to ascend with him. With him not in the sense of walking beside him or after him. With him in the sense of sacramental assimilation to him. It makes sense, in other words, to talk not just about Jesus the person but about Jesus the sacrament. Existing independently of him, his achievement in the Karmic Canyon, drinking from the cup and the skull within

it, is an inheritance we can appropriate into the roots and auroras of who we are. Alternatively, we might say that much as the metamorphic principle is in insects so is the Christ principle in us. Dormant perhaps for life-times, when it eventually awakens and becomes active in us, there is little we can do but go with it, crossing the Torrent into Gethsemane and onward to Golgotha.

Reassured that God is with us, however insensibly, we continue our ascent.

To Al-Niffari, the great Muslim mystic, God said:

> Between Me and thee is thy self-experience. Cast it from thee and I will veil thee from thyself.

And Al-Hallaj, another great Muslim mystic – this is how he prayed to God:

> Between me and Thee there is an 'I am' that torments me. Ah! through Thy 'I am' take away my 'I am' from between us both.

A privy counsellor to us in our ascent, the author of The Cloud of Unknowing puts it this way:

> And this is the trewe condicion of a parfit lover, only and utterly to spoyle hym-self of him-self for that thing that he lovith, and not admit ne suffer to be clothed bot only in that thing that he lovith; and that not only for a tyme, bot eendlesly to be umbilappid therin, in ful and final forgetyng of hym-self.

At noon on Golgotha, a nunatak rising above dualizing mind within the Canyon, the seeker self-absent, it happens to those to whom God is gracious.

Here is how Eckhart describes what happens:

> Comes then the soul into the unclouded light of God. It is transported so far from creaturehood into nothingness that, of its own powers, it can never return to its sensory and intellectual agencies or to its former creaturehood. Once there, God shelters the soul's nothingness with his uncreated essence, safeguarding its creaturely existence. The soul has dared to become nothing, and cannot pass from its own being into nothingness and then back again, losing its own identity in the process, except God safeguarded it. This must needs be so.

This is how Henry Suso describes it:

> When the soul, forgetting itself, dwells in that radiant darkness, it loses all its faculties and all its qualities, as St. Bernard has said. And this, more or less completely, according to whether the soul - whether in the body or out of the body – is more or less united to God. This forgetfulness of self is, in a measure, a transformation in God; who then becomes, in a certain manner, all things for the soul, as Scripture saith. In this rapture the soul disappears, but not yet entirely. It acquires, it is true, certain qualities of Divinity, but does not naturally become divine ... To speak in the common language, the soul is rapt, by the divine power of resplendent Being, above its natural faculties, into the nakedness of the Nothing.

Elsewhere he says:

> When the good and faithful servant enters into the joy of his Lord, he is inebriated by the riches of the house of God; for he feels, in an ineffable degree, that which is felt by an inebriated man. He forgets himself, he is no longer conscious of his selfhood; he disappears and loses himself in God, and becomes one spirit with Him, as a drop of water which is drowned in a great quantity of wine. For even as such a drop disappears, taking the colour and taste of wine, so it is with those who are in full possession of blessedness ...

Having talked about being well and truly drunk on what she hasn't drunk and never will be able to drink, and her ascending soul having fallen from love to nothingness, Marguerite Porete alludes in passing to the state of

Being in God without being oneself

That in no sense a description of indescribable

Final Glory

A Monastic Settlement

Called

Slí na Fírinne

Ethos and Rule

At the centre

During the ritual called Tenebrae

A Tenebrae harrow

Nine branched, it is

our

Little Yggdrasil

our

Burning Bush

our

Bodhi tree

At the centre

During the ritual called Ephphatha

A silver branch

In performing Tenebrae, we are attempting to stay awake with Jesus from the moment he crosses the Torrent until the moment he reappears in the Garden of the Sepulchre.

In vestibules either side of the door into the sanctuary we invest ourselves in our megalonschemas. In this we are symbolically inheriting our baptism, our best hope of divine safekeeping throughout.

Entering the sanctuary, we sit around the harrow, we light the nine candles and we begin.

In this house our hope is to prosper in pioneering prayer with Jesus.

It is for each individual to choose whether to watch with him, to walk with him or to grow in sacramental assimilation to him in enduring and doing.

Scripted and scored as an oratorio, Tenebrae will give the impression all the way through of Jubilation, sometimes desperate Jubilation, but Jubilation nonetheless. It is after all the next greatest thing since the coming forth of the world that we are celebrating.

In Ephphatha we are aware that silver branch perception is Paradisal perception regained.

THE MONASTIC DAY

Structured around three periods of chanted prayer and silent meditation:

7.00 – 8.00 a.m.
12.30 – 1.00 p.m.
6.00 – 7.00 p.m.

On Saturday nights, from midnight, Tenebrae will be performed.
On Sunday mornings we will perform Ephphatha.
Believing that nature is relevation not veil we will spend time sacramentally alone in its great solitudes.
Whether inside or outside, work will be as little industrialized as possible.
Big engine sounds will be as rarely heard as possible.
Wherever possible, primitive tools not power tools.
Blackbird's eggs haven't had the time to adapt to modern mechanical noise, haven't had the time to soundproof themselves against the revving roars and the roaring drone of a chainsaw.
Ours is a house in a wood.
A wood you might meet Merlin in.
A wood Bran Mac Feabhail might have retired to.
Meet Bran in our wood and he will tell you that in every branch is the music of the Silver Branch.
The ethos of our house is in its hallows. They are:

The karmic digging fork
The Tenebrae harrow
The silver branch

As we practice it, the adventure of our immortality includes and is kind to the adventure of our mortality.
It is our belief that Jesus has claimed the whole psyche for sanctity.
Nothing of what we are will be left behind on the purgatorial dancing floor. Our monastic day reflects and expresses our beliefs.